Praise for *The Reali*

"... a tool for bringing mind, brain, and body into alignment, that we might be at peace with ourselves and so with others...personal rewards are endless."

Joseph Chilton Pearce
author of *Crack in the Cosmic Egg*

"...unusually clear, accessible account of the mysteries of the multidimensional world."

Marilyn Ferguson
author of *The Aquarian Conspiracy*

"A powerful learning tool...a clear guide for taking an important step towards an enlarged way of perceiving our lives."

Timothy Gallwey
author of *The Inner Game of Tennis*

"Physics and metaphysics...a bold attempt at synthesis."

Thelma Moss
author of *The Probability of the Impossible*

"...takes you to the boundaries of your own mind and occasionally makes you gasp with wonder at glimpses of what lies beyond"

Serge King
author of *Kahuna Healing*

"An important contribution to brain/mind and how reality is viewed."

Joan Halifax
author of *Shamanic Voice*

About the Author

Ralph Strauch lives in Pacific Palisades, California, where he teaches and writes about self-awareness, movement, and the mechanisms through which we create and organize our experience. He has been exploring the relationship between perception and reality for more than 30 years, drawing on his background as a martial artist and mathematician as well as on his training and experience as a *Feldenkrais Teacher*.

After receiving his Ph.D. in Statistics from the University of California, Ralph spent 15 years as a Senior Mathematician with the Rand Corporation. His research at Rand focused on issues of human and organizational decisionmaking. His interests in perception and bodymind interaction grew out of that research, in combination with his experiences in the martial arts of *T'ai Chi* and *Aikido* and personal explorations which followed from them.

Ralph subsequently studied with Moshe Feldenkrais, the Israeli physicist who developed the *Feldenkrais Method* of somatic education. He now maintains a private practice as a *Feldenkrais Teacher*.

The Reality Illusion

How you make the world you experience

by
Ralph Strauch

with a foreword by
Joseph Chilton Pearce

Somatic
Options™
...to live more fully
in your body

To Merna
for your part in it all

The Reality Illusion

How you make the world you experience

by Ralph Strauch

©1983, 1989 by Ralph Strauch

Illustrations by Katarzyna Kozik and Merna Strauch

Cover photo by Ralph Strauch

Originally published by Quest Books, Wheaton, IL 1983

This edition published 2000 by **Somatic Options**
1383 Avenida de Cortez, Pacific Palisades, CA 90272
Email: books@somatic.com
www.somatic.com

ISBN 0-9676009-3-6

Library of Congress Card Number 99-91934

Printed in the United States of America

Contents

Preface

It's been over a decade since I began work on *The Reality Illusion*, and six years since the first edition was published. During that time, a revolution has taken place in the public acceptance of such ideas. A decade ago these ideas were beginning to creep into the fringes of public consciousness. Today they are still outside the mainstream, but the interest in and acceptability of them has grown considerably. This growth appears to be an ongoing natural process, as people seek a deeper understanding of their place in the world than the Western intellectual worldview can provide.

The ideas that we create our own reality and are responsible for our own experience are powerful ones. Opening new possibilities, they also raise new and sometimes troubling questions. Two issues, in particular, are often confusing to people attempting to assimilate these concepts. One concerns the role that a separate external reality plays in our experience, and the other concerns the levels at which we make choices and the relationship between our choices and the outcomes they produce.

WHAT IS IT WE CREATE?

As you begin to contemplate the possibility that you are responsible for more of your own experience than you had heretofore realized, you may wonder if that means that you are the sole creator of all experience. "If I create reality," you may ask, "does that mean reality exists only in my mind? Are all the situations I face and the people I meet only products of my imagination, with no reality beyond that which I give them?"

The resolution of this apparent conundrum lies, I believe, in understanding the difference between creating *reality* and creating *your experience of reality*. You create your personal experience of reality—that is to say, your individual way of seeing, interpreting, and interacting with the world around you. But you do not create that experience in a vacuum. There is a rich external reality "out there" independent of you, from which you filter and select the particular pattern of experience that becomes your personal reality.

The people in your life are not your creations; they are separate beings each as powerful and autonomous as you. You create *your experience* of them, just as each of them creates his or her experience of you. You have no real power over who anyone else is or what they do, only over how you experience and interact with them. But how you (and they) exercise that power to interact can create the illusion of the power to control. If I unconsciously limit my actions based on what you do or what I think you might do, for example, I create the illusion (for both of us) that you have control over me.

An acquaintance who was very much involved with the *est* training, which teaches similar concepts, once told me about a promotional gathering she had arranged to recruit people for *est*. Her meeting had produced no recruits, and that troubled her. She had really wanted those people to take the *est* training, she told me, and the fact that none of them did was making her question whether or not she really could create her own reality.

It was clear, as I listened to her, that she was confusing her ability to create *her* reality with her ability (or lack thereof) to create *their* realities. Each of them had, for whatever reasons, decided not to take the "opportunity" she offered them. Rather than accepting that and examining what it had to teach her (about the way she presented *est*, perhaps), she chose to feel upset and inadequate, and to waste her time in pointless metaphysical speculation about whether or not that experience negated her new beliefs. Everyone else you meet possesses the same abilities that you do, and deserves respect as an equally autonomous being.

Experience consists of two components—*events* occurring in the external world, and your *interpretation of and interaction with* those events. The events do exist "out there," independent of you, and you have *direct* control only over your interpretation of and interaction with them. That gives you considerable *indirect* control over the events themselves, however, because the world as a whole is a responsive and interactive place. Those external events are themselves made up of others' responses to your actions, etc., and so are affected by your responses to them. But whatever the events, your ability to change your interpretation of and interaction with them can give you tremendous control over the way you experience them.

This can be clearly seen in the experiences of Jacques Lusseyran, described in his book *And There Was Light.* Blinded in an accident at the age of eight, Lusseyran did not choose to become demoralized and see himself as "disabled." Instead, he accepted his impairment as a gift, and developed a far richer and more sensitive awareness of the world around him than those of us hampered by the distractions of vision usually bother to achieve. As a teenage leader in the French Resistance during World War II, he employed his highly developed sensitivity to screen prospective recruits and weed out those who felt untrustworthy or unreliable to him. The one man he accepted in spite of his intuitive reservations later betrayed his organization to the Gestapo.

He was sent to the concentration camp at Buchenwald, where conditions were horrible and he became extremely ill. No medical treatment was available and his friends expected him to die. But in the midst of his illness he found tranquility. He recovered, and spent the next eleven months (until the camp was liberated) in a state of calm serenity. In that state, he was a source of comfort and peace to others in the camp. Out of two thousand Resistance fighters who accompanied him to Buchenwald, he was one of thirty survivors.

This example is extreme, but does illustrate the power to learn and grow even from the worst of external circumstances.

LEVELS OF CHOICE

Another issue which creates confusion concerns the levels at which we make the choices that determine our experience. "If we create our own reality," some people reason, "then someone who gets sick, has an accident, or experiences some other calamity must have subconsciously chosen that particular outcome." This line of reasoning is wrong, confusing control of the mechanisms that produce experience with prior knowledge of the outcomes they will produce. I can drive my car along a road without knowing where that road goes, or having any subconscious reason to get to whatever lies at its end.

We make choices at different levels, and many of the choices that significantly influence our experience are subconscious and automatic, controlled by habitual reflexes well below the level of consciousness. We install these habitual reflexes over long periods of time in many different situations and apply them automatically without considering their consequences in any particular situation. Indeed, we are often unaware that there are even any alternatives, though in fact there always are.

When someone gets sick or has an accident, that sickness

or accident is the consequence of choices they have made which they could have made differently. But that does not necessarily mean that they "chose" that particular outcome. It may have come about simply as a consequence of the pattern of activity by which they organize their life.

Consider an example discussed in more detail in Chapter 9. If you accidently touch a live wire and suffer a severe electrical shock, that doesn't necessarily mean that you subconsciously wanted that shock. But you did interact with the world (as most of us do) by tensing and contracting against the external stimulus as a way of defending against it. When you come in contact with a live wire, this maximizes the shock you receive. Similarly, contracting cancer may not imply a subconscious choice to get cancer so much as a habitual withdrawal of awareness from the area where the cancer develops, denying that area the efficient mobilization of the body's normal defense mechanisms (Chapter 8).

Understanding that experience arises as the consequence of low level, habitual patterns of behavior is important, because it points the way to effective avenues for change. It is not enough to "purify your thoughts" and wish for positive change. You must broaden your awareness to become cognizant of the habitual patterns of microbehavior that organize and structure your interactions with the world around you. Only then can you take control of those patterns and change them in ways that serve you better. I hope this book will help you to do that.

MY OWN ONGOING PATH

My life continues along a path of exploration and learning. In 1980 I met Moshe Feldenkrais, an Israeli physicist who developed a revolutionary system for exploring and reeducating the neuromuscular patterning which determines our movements and kinesthetic perceptions. In his work I found an extraordinary tool for exploring the questions that drive my life, so I began to study with him. I have left the world of mathematics and military systems analysis altogether, and now work as a Feldenkrais Teacher.

My life continues to revolve around deepening my understanding of the mechanisms through which we create and maintain our ongoing flow of experience, and helping others to utilize those mechanisms in ways that serve them better. My recent focus has been on the neuromuscular mechanisms through which we act in the world, and on the nature of the feeling process and the ways that contemporary society suppresses and distorts it. As my understanding deepens, it continues to reinforce the basic soundness of the insights on which *The Reality Illusion* was based.

RALPH STRAUCH
October, 1988
Pacific Palisades, California

Foreword

Recent research shows that we have, within our skulls, not one but three separate and distinct brains. Paul McLean calls these the reptilian, old mammalian, and new mammalian (or human) brains. He points out that they are the major brain systems developed throughout evolutionary history, that we carry the whole story in our heads.

Our ongoing dilemma and current social collapse arise, McLean believes (as do physicist David Bohm and others) from a lack of communication between our two "animal brains" and our all-too-human "thinking brain." The mythological figure of the *centaur*, a human with an animal body, depicts this split. For untold millenia that monolithic giant of the deserts, the Sphinx, has sat as a reminder that we are a human head resting on an animal body; that our thinking grows out of and critically depends on the support of animal brain functions.

We deny or forget this fact continually and at severe cost. Our mind/brain and body are designed to function as an integral unit. Integration is developmental, however, and development can break down. When it does, the breakdown tends to get *handed down* from generation to generation. We have inherited a breakdown between our "animal" and "human" brains, and this breakdown breeds the anxiety of a faulty perception and a split intellect.

An avalanche of remedies for our current state engulfs us— but most only add to our chaos and confusion. Indeed, social solutions are huckstered about in profusion, with no *hint* of what our problem is.

Ralph Strauch invites us to examine the root cause of our perennial discord and disarray. If we, as readers, are willing to look at our lives from the position, from the question he posits, we will comprehend the nature of the answer we need—an answer admirably approached within this book.

I met Ralph Strauch some years ago and found him an integrated individual; one without pretense or facade, a person centered in the moment and operating in open non-defensive honesty and a calm, clear intelligence. These are rare traits and Ralph proves to be a rare combination. On the one hand he holds a doctorate in mathematics and was long an integral part of a famous "think-tank" involved in national decisionmaking; on the other hand, he has been for years a student of oriental disciplines, particularly the martial arts. Ralph demonstrates, in his life, a striking example of intellectual development balanced by the intense body-mind discipline and coordination demanded by those martial arts. As George Leonard beautifully described in *The Silent Pulse*, Ralph reflects the balance of the *centaur*.

This book reflects that balance, for no one can write effectively and convincingly of a state he has not grasped.

I have found that as readers or listeners we hear an answer only when we have understood the issue and can seriously join in asking the question. In the pages that follow we are challenged to move beyond our shallow automatic assumptions and examine the nature of our personal awareness. We are led to a serious questioning of perception and consciousness—questioning which opens us to the possibility of a transformative answer, one beyond our previous knowing.

Though unique in approach, the answer Ralph gives is of necessity similar to that given by others—for there is only one basic question, and only one answer. Here, though, we also find practical and reasonable exercises which give a tangible basis for serious transformative work on ourselves. These exercises are not just syntheses of ancient disciplines and current popular practices. They are intelligent methods distinctly appropriate for inclusion in our fast-paced, time-bound lives.

Ralph's work is a tool for bringing mind, brain, and body into alignment, that we might be at peace with ourselves and so with others. The alignment of human and animal functions gives harmony within and dominion over the world without.

Our current social madness can be redressed only through such individual transformation as can be found here. No one is going to legislate our current crises away. Each of us must assume responsibility for changing our own life, for bringing inner and outer into balance. This requires new insights, some discipline and guidance. The whole person is the only one through whom social change can be affected. Ralph's book points us toward this state and invites us to actualize it in our lives. Cultural survival may well depend upon such action; personal survival surely does. And the peripheral personal rewards are endless.

JOSEPH CHILTON PEARCE

Introduction

Look around you. What do you see? A room, some furniture, a window through which you can see outside? Or perhaps, if you have picked up this book while browsing, a bookstore filled with books and other shoppers. Wherever you are, you see a material world containing solid material objects—people and things. That's what you see because that's what's out there and your eyes present you with an objective picture of the world around you. At least that's the way we tell ourselves it is. "Seeing is believing," after all.

But it's not really that way at all. The things you see when you look around you are not "out there." They are pictures in your head, images you make up and play for yourself. So are the sounds you hear, the smells you smell, and even the weight and solidity you feel. You produce them all yourself. You create your own perceptions, and through them your own reality. The world you think of as "out there" is not separate and external at all, but is instead your *reality illusion*.

This is not to say that external reality does not exist. It does, and is far richer and more complex than most people ever imagine. You don't perceive that external reality, however, in

1

anything approaching its totality. Rather, you get partial, incomplete, and distorted impressions, constructed from selected fragments of the external world and your expectations, preexisting beliefs, and past experience. The reality you inhabit is your own construction—a product of the way you filter, interpret and select from the infinite range of possibilities available.

This view of reality differs from the currently dominant Western world-view which holds that an "objective" external reality does exist, independent of the knower yet capable of being accurately described by science. The Western world-view recognizes that the perceptual processes of individuals are fallible and subject to illusion and misperception. It contends, however, that these individual fallibilities can be overcome collectively through science and the scientific method, and that the picture of reality thus obtained will ever more closely approximate what is actually "out there."

Trained as a Western scientist, I accepted that world-view for most of my life. I came to question it, however, and I now believe it to be fundamentally wrong. This book attempts to articulate my current beliefs, and some of the evidence, logic and experience on which they rest.

The relationship between external reality and our perceptions of it can be likened to the relationship between an object, such as a car, and a picture of that object. The picture may represent some aspects of the object very well. This picture, for example, shows the general lines of the car quite clearly. It shows the shape of the hood, the number of headlights, and the fact that the car has a front bumper. But there are also aspects which the picture represents poorly or actually distorts. This picture tells us nothing about the color of the car, what the tail lights look like, or what the car is like internally. The relative length and width are badly distorted, in that the two front wheels in the picture are much further apart than the front and rear wheels, while the car is actually longer than it is wide. We hardly notice this distortion, however, because our familiarity with cars and with perspective representation allows us to interpret the picture without difficulty.

We often blur the distinction between the object and the

picture—as when we say, for example, "I have a car like this," or "This car gets good gas mileage." We know, nonetheless, that the picture is not the object, and we are not likely to be confused about the distinction. We would not buy the picture for the price of the car. The picture represents the object but does not duplicate it, in part because the three-dimensional nature of the object is so much richer than the two-dimensional nature of the picture.

Now think about external reality, whatever that might be, as corresponding to the object, and of any perception or intellectual description of reality as corresponding to the picture. Just as the picture is inherently incapable of fully characterizing the object, so is the human mind incapable of fully comprehending external reality. Any perception will necessarily be partial and incomplete, distorting important aspects of reality just as the picture distorts aspects of the object. This may not appear self-evident right now, but I hope to convince you of it by the time you finish reading this book.

Many different pictures can be made of any given object. Photographs can be taken from different perspectives; line drawings or schematics can be made, even caricatures of various kinds. Each may validly represent the object, though the pictures themselves may be quite different. No single picture can be said to be "better" than all others in any absolute terms.

So it is with descriptions of reality. There are many different *Reality* ways of understanding and experiencing reality, and it may appear quite different from different perspectives. Superficially contradictory descriptions may be equally valid (like pictures taken from different perspectives) and no single description will be better than all others in absolute terms.

A single object will look different from different perspectives and the converse is also true. The same image may be seen as very different objects. The ambiguous face/vase reversing figure shown below provides a classic example. The drawing can be seen as a black vase against a white background, or as two white faces turned toward each other against a black background. The foreground of one interpretation becomes the background of the other and vice versa. You can see either interpretation and can switch from one to the other at will.

Try it a few times. Switch back and forth and attend to the change as you do so. With a little practice you can begin to notice the switch taking place. Perhaps you can even catch the little "click" in your head as it happens. One explanation says that ambiguous figures of this sort arise because we resolve figure/ground differentiations (i.e., distinguish between objects and their backgrounds) in more than one way. But there seems to be something more than figure/ground differentiation involved here. Look at another ambiguous figure which seems quite similar to the faces/vase but does not involve different figure/ground interpretations.°

12
A 13 C
14

What is the character in the middle of the figure? Read across and it looks like a B. Read down and it's clearly a 13. Which is it? Or is it neither? Or both? It doesn't seem to be both, at least in the sense that you can see it as both at the same time. It's one or the other and you can switch easily by changing the context you see it in—but it's never both at the same time. Unlike the faces/vase, no figure/ground shift is involved—no change in the way the contours are seen. The difference lies only in the way those contours are given meaning by the mind, yet the fact that we see something very different in each context is unassailable. And as before, if you watch the process closely as you switch back and forth, you can notice the little "click" in your head as the switch occurs.

These illustrations involve the visual perception of relatively simple visual stimuli, but the parallels with our broader perceptions of the world should be obvious. Just as reality may look quite different when we perceive it from different viewpoints, *Reality* so may we interpret a single perspective—a fixed set of data—in different ways. What we see will be affected by what we take as primary (the figure/ground differentiation we make) as well as by the context we see it in (reading across or up-and-down).

°The illustration is from Robert Ornstein's *The Psychology of Consciousness* (New York: Viking, Penguin Books, 1975), reprinted by permission of the publisher.

The same "facts" may thus appear quite different to different people, or even to the same person at different times or in different contexts.

If not carried too far, these ideas seem relatively benign and hardly at variance with commonly accepted Western knowledge. Most people know that economists see a world made up of economic transactions, while dentists see a collection of people having problems with their teeth. Anthropologists talk of "cultural relativity," and the better that science understands the "objective world," the clearer it becomes that different people see the world differently.

But what of that "objective world" described by science? The analogy cannot apply to that, or can it? Many who would accept the relativity of the economist or dentist would argue that the same thing is not true of the physicist or the chemist. They would claim that physical and chemical properties of the world are "real" in the sense that they derive from objective "laws of nature," independent of the observer and how he sees the situation. "Fire can burn you whether you believe in it or not," they might argue, and "the law of gravity cannot be broken."

Yet there do appear to be exceptions. Fire burns most people most of the time, but firewalking is common in cultures throughout the world. Often as part of a religious ritual, groups of devotees walk over beds of red-hot coals without suffering ill effects. Closer to home, ordinary people sometimes perform feats well beyond their "normal" capabilities under situations of extreme stress. A few years ago in San Diego, a twelve year old boy lifted a car which had slipped off a jack while his father was underneath it. Later he could not budge the car. People under the influence of drugs sometimes do things which seem to violate the usual "laws of physics." A man in San Francisco survived a twenty story fall with nothing worse than two broken ankles. Could such phenomena be explained in terms of altered perceptions, allowing interactions with the world not possible in "ordinary reality?"

What about "faith healers" and others with "paranormal" capabilities? Do such abilities, perhaps, result from different ways of perceiving? Lawrence LeShan, author of *The Medium, the Mystic, and the Physicist*, has examined the accounts of mediums and healers concerning their state of mind while they "do their thing," and concludes that they perceive the world in a basically different way than the rest of us. Most of us, most of the time, see the world in ways which emphasize the separateness of things—particularly the separation between ourselves and the rest of the world. The medium or the healer, on the other hand, sees a unity to all things. The process of healing occurs, LeShan feels, when the healer transfers this perception of oneness to the patient.

I believe that LeShan is basically correct, and that these phenomena can be explained and understood in perceptual terms. We see and understand only part of the world, and our interactions reflect partial understanding. If we perceive the world differently, we live in a different world where different interactions become possible. Any single picture of the world is incomplete—that of the physicist or the chemist as much as that of the dentist or the economist. The same mechanisms limit the view of the physicist which limit the view of the dentist— claims about the "objectivity of science" notwithstanding. This book will explore these mechanisms and the images of reality we create using them.

In doing this, I will try to stretch your mind. I will ask you to imagine how a dolphin might think, how the world might seem if we were totally insensitive to temperature, or how reality might look if we thought about it in a language with a different structure. I will give you exercises to show you aspects of your interactions with the world which you may not have seen before, and which your ego works very hard to keep you from seeing. This may be strange, uncomfortable and perhaps difficult at times; but if you stick with it, it should be rewarding and even fun.

We each inhabit our own reality, a reality largely of our own making. The appearance of a common external "objective reality" results from the high degree of agreement between our individual realities. But this agreement stems from the fact that we learn as we mature to see the world the same way those around us do. We teach our children to see it the same way, thus perpetuating the agreement. That agreement, rather than resulting from the existence of an "objective reality," is the source of the illusion that such a reality exists.

Several years ago I discussed some of these ideas with a physicist I knew. I told him that I was beginning to take seriously the possibility that the world was quite different from what we usually perceive, and from what we describe in our scientific theories and models. I tried to show him, with both verbal and experiential examples, some of the tricks we play on ourselves to maintain our consensus reality. He dismissed each example by finding a way of explaining it within the consensus reality framework, or by holding that my facts were wrong or that I was misinterpreting them. I finally asked him if he thought that men had ever walked on the moon.

"Of course," he said.

"How do you know?"

"I watched it on TV."

"How do you know it was real? There are a dozen Hollywood studios which could have produced that footage, and even have done it better."

He thought about that for a moment, then jokingly observed that the poor quality of some of the transmissions from the moon was itself evidence of their veracity. A simulation would have been better. I said that that was rather weak evidence. He agreed, but said he had once been to the Kennedy Space Center and seen one of the moon rockets which certainly seemed capable of taking a man to the moon. He admitted, however, that he had never seen one take off, and that even if he had he could not be sure that it actually went to the moon.

He finally admitted that he had no *direct* way of verifying that men had actually walked on the moon. His belief that it had happened was based on accepting the reports of others. He still felt that he could personally be sure of such things as man-made satellites circling the earth, and offered the live TV coverage of sporting events from Europe as evidence. He felt he understood the physical mechanisms involved well enough to know that only a communications satellite could provide coverage as good as he had witnessed.

"How do you know it was live?" I asked.

At this, he lost patience with the verbal games we were playing. "Look," he replied, "you can always undercut or refute any particular piece of evidence. But there are hundreds of pieces, things I know about physics and about technology. It's not any one piece that matters. It's the whole pattern, the way it all fits together."

That was exactly my point!

I was not trying to question the fact that men had walked on the moon, or to suggest that he should doubt it in the least. I did want to show him, though, that his knowledge of that event was not based on a few isolatable and easily verifiable "facts." Rather, it rested on a complex and interlocking network of knowledge and belief that fits together as a whole, even though each isolated piece can be questioned. The same was true of the perspective I was trying to show him, which he had been rejecting on a point-by-point basis as I went along.

This holds true for the arguments presented in this book. You will read things you may not have contacted before and be asked to look at familiar facts in unfamiliar ways. No single piece of evidence will "refute" consensus reality by itself, or "prove" the viewpoint I claim it supports. If you read the book with an attitude of skepticism, determined to defend consensus reality and to require hard "proof" for every departure therefrom, you will find your doubts easily vindicated. The individual pieces of evidence, taken separately, may be readily given alternative explanations.

What matters, however, are not the individual pieces but the overall gestalt into which they fit, and I can only show you that gestalt a piece at a time. Before you can see the overall pattern, you must allow enough individual pieces to accumulate to make the pattern visible. This may require a "suspension of disbelief" as portions of the argument are presented, as distinct from the constantly critical and questioning attitude which is often so useful in scientific work and academic scholarship.

This book is not a work of scholarship in the academic sense. It does not purport to convey "objective" information about an "objective" world. Rather, it attempts to articulate a highly personal perspective on how the world works, and to make that perspective and the foundation on which it rests available to you. This disclaimer is not an apology, simply an explanation. It should become clear as we proceed that I believe the subjects addressed here—the nature of reality and our perceptions of it—to be subjects which the tools of conventional scholarship and scientific investigation are ill equipped to address.

This book is a personal perspective; the ideas in it have been strongly influenced by my unique life stream. I see the world the way I do because of my particular background and experience and the lessons I have drawn from them. Three important aspects of that background have been my training as a mathematician, my career as a systems and policy analyst, and my interests in the Oriental martial arts and the philosophies and mental disciplines related to them. I was trained as a theoretical mathematician specializing in probability theory and statistics. I learned to be comfortable with the idea of abstract mathematical models as entities in their own right, with independent structure and existence of their own, apart from that of any physical reality they might serve to describe. These ideas later extended naturally to the more general "models" of reality discussed later in the book.

One of the core ideas I had to assimilate was that of mathematical "probability space" representing the universe of possible outcomes of some process under consideration. Which one would be actually realized could never be known directly but only inferred from the values of observed "random variables." Much of probability theory and statistics is concerned with how this can be done. This sounds like a complex and abstract set of ideas, foreign to most people's realm of experience, and it is. The most difficult part of my scientific education was assimilating these ideas intuitively. I eventually did, and found that mathematical arguments which had previously been formal chains of logic without intuitive content suddenly made sense, clearly and quite independently of the formal logic involved. This gave me a new appreciation for mathematics as an intuitive activity in which the formal proofs and chains of reasoning, which most people think of as primary, play a distinctly secondary (though still important) role.

Two aspects of this are relevant here. One involves the content of some of these ideas, while the other concerns the way I internalized them. The first involves the concept of an underlying process which can never be observed directly but only through its effects. Though I internalized this idea as a characteristic of mathematical probability spaces, it proved to be useful in thinking about other things as well. Eventually I came to see it as a useful way of thinking about reality as a whole, and it plays an important role in the view of perception and reality presented in this book.

#2

The second insight concerned the role an individual's internal gestalt plays in his perception of the world around him. My shift in understanding occurred slowly enough that I was able to see it occurring. Ideas became clear and intuitive which had previously been incomprehensible or understood only as bland formal truths without intuitive content. But the ideas hadn't changed, nor had the words describing them. The change had been in me, in the way I perceived and related to the ideas. As the years went by, I saw repeatedly how strongly an individual's ability to understand or even to consider an idea was dependent on the gestalt with which he responded to it.

After graduate school I went to work for the Rand Corporation, a prestigious California "think tank" which at that time (mid 1960s) did research primarily for the United States Air Force. I engaged in the kinds of research activities which go under labels like systems analysis, operations research, and policy analysis. One of my major research concerns there was with methodology and the way it was used—with the kinds of models analysts employed and the ways they interpreted results obtained using those models. That was the context, in fact, in which the ideas about perception expressed in this book first began to take shape.

I went to Rand as a "true believer" in the promise of systems analysis—intellectually committed to the idea that "war was too important to leave to the generals" and to the belief that the application of mathematical reasoning to military and social problems could make the world a safer and better place. With time, however, that belief began to tarnish as I saw analyses performed in ways which often served to cloud important issues rather than to illuminate them. At first I thought I was seeing problems in the application of basically sound ideas—sloppy procedures which could be easily corrected with a little care and watchfulness on the part of the practitioners. I later came to see them as deeper and more fundamental deficiencies in the methodologies employed and in the mindsets of those who employed them.

I eventually came to see the fundamental issues involved as issues of perception. The images of the world held by believers in the magic of systems analysis were shaped by the models they employed. Factors which were quantifiable would come into clear, sharp focus while unquantifiable factors would be defocused, to fade unnoticed into the background. Models of warfare, for example, treat it as a mechanical interaction between opposing forces in which such factors as military leadership and the quality and morale of the opposing troops played no role, in spite of their historical importance in actual warfare. This led me to think about perception in general and the importance of the models through which perception is filtered and organized.

I originally became interested in the martial arts as a recreational activity. They provided a good way to keep in shape, and it seemed that a few self-defense skills could never be bad to have. I spent several months with karate, followed by a couple of years with judo and ju-jitsu. Eventually I found my way into T'ai Chi and Aikido, both "internal" martial arts stressing relaxation and self-awareness and a yielding, redirecting approach to external conflict. Both teach awareness and control of a life force or energy, termed *Ch'i* by the Chinese and *Ki* by the Japanese. Descriptions of this energy and what can be done with it sound esoteric and somewhat superstitious to Western ears. T'ai Chi adepts who have fully mastered the art (and there are very few) are reputed to be almost invincible and capable of seemingly superhuman feats.

I came to realize that here was really something beyond the scope of my previous understanding, something real and interesting enough to be worth seriously exploring. This led me into Taoist and Buddhist philosophy and meditation, and to the works of writers like Carlos Castaneda and Joseph Pearce. I found well-established and internally consistent systems of thought quite different from the positivist Western world-view within which I had been educated, systems with important things to say about aspects of human experience largely ignored by the contemporary mainstream of Western thought.

The perspectives I obtained from these sources comple-
mented the ideas to which my thinking about mathematics and
models had led me. Each reinforced the other, giving me
insights which I would not have had from either alone. The
combination of the intellectual (from reading and thinking)
with the experiential (from meditation and the martial arts)
was also complementary and served to enhance the value of
both components. My martial arts experience led to new ways of
exploring the nature of perception and physical interaction to
depths I had not previously known. These explorations were the
source of much insight, and of many of the experiential exercises
described later in the book. Eventually I came to see these
diverse sources of ideas and experiences as different perspectives on a common theme—the nature of our perceptual
processes and the images of reality we use those processes to
create and maintain. This book is an attempt to articulate that
theme and some of the experience which led me to it.

1

The Nature of Perception

We know the world around us in many different ways. We see, hear, touch, taste and smell it through the ordinary five senses. Through our kinesthetic sense we are aware of our position in space and of the movement of our body. Our "sense of balance" orients us to the vertical through sensing mechanisms in our inner ear. Beyond these direct and continuing perceptions of our immediate surroundings, we know less immediate aspects of the world with our intellect. I will refer to this "knowing about" kind of knowing as *intellectual perception* in contrast to the more direct and immediate *experiential perception* provided by the senses. This distinction is less sharp than it might first appear, but can be useful nonetheless.

It is worth noting, perhaps, that I am using the term *perception* more broadly than it is often used. Many writers would apply the term only to what we get from our senses—even less than what I am calling *experiential perception*—and would use other terms like cognition, knowing, reasoning, and homeostasis to describe things which I include within the term *perception*. This is less a matter of disagreement, I think, than of difference in focus. There are differences between the processes of vision and of reasoning, and there are similarities. If you are interested in the differences, it makes sense to define your terms in ways which emphasize those differences—to say that vision is perception and reasoning is cognition, and perception and cognition are different. I am interested in the similarities, so it makes sense to consider them both as aspects of a larger common process. I am calling this common larger process perception.

There are precedents for using the term *perception* in this broader sense. Eastern, and especially Buddhist, writings, seem to adopt this viewpoint when they classify the intellect as the "sixth sense." Ordinary language recognizes the commonalities by using terms like *see* ("see what I mean") and *image* (your image of these ideas) to refer to intellectual understanding as well as to vision. Each of these forms of perception, and others we'll examine later as well, is an image-forming process. Each provides the perceiver employing them (think of yourself) with images of portions of his or her environment. Vision provides visual images of the surroundings, while hearing provides auditory images of sounds produced nearby. Intellectual perception provides conceptual images of many things, including people, nations, political parties, and trees; and of the sundry relationships existing between those things.

As a first approximation of what I mean by an image-forming process, think about taking a picture of some object. The thing being perceived corresponds to the object, the perceptual image of it to the image on the film, and the perceptual mechanism producing it to the things which produce the picture—the lens through which the image is formed, the film which records the image, etc.

As noted earlier, this simple analogy illustrates several important aspects of perception in general. The most important, perhaps, is the fact that the image only partially and incompletely represents the object, in a manner which depends significantly on the perspective from which it was made. Images from different perspectives may look quite different, even though they each validly represent the same object. This analogy also has serious weaknesses. The picture is formed when light reflecting from the object passes through the lens to the film. The lens casts an objective image, which the film simply records as the pattern of light and dark (and possibly color) reflected from the object. The simple "eye as a camera" model which most of us learned in school describes vision in much the same way, with the image formed on the retina of the eye then transmitted along the optic nerve to the brain as an objective representation of the scene we are viewing. But that model is wrong; vision is much more complex.

When we look out at the world around us, we see *things*— objects and events in our visual environment—not patterns of light and dark. You see this book as a *book*, separate and distinct from the background, and not as part of an optical pattern with that background. You see the print as letters, words, and phrases—not as optical patterns. That is why the B and the 13 in the ambiguous figure look different, even though the optical pattern is the same. You are hardly aware of the details of the pattern itself, unless it is specifically brought to your attention. Ask yourself, for example, if the A in the ambiguous figure was solid or had a split in it, then look back and see if you are right.

The other senses work similarly. You hear the sound of *something*, not the raw acoustic pattern impinging on your ears. You feel the solidity of the chair you are sitting on as you read, not the tactile pattern of that chair against your body. Even your intellectual perceptions consist of summary concepts and con- clusions, rather than of the specific patterns of information and experience from which those conclusions were formed.

Think about a sketch made by an artist in contrast to the kind of picture a camera makes. It is an interpretative picture, not a direct optical image. The artist does not record everything she sees, but selects particular elements of the scene and reproduces them according to personal style and the effect being attempted. To sketch a boat, she includes details necessary to her idea of that boat and ignores most of the detail actually there "ob- jectively." The end result may look quite different from a photograph, yet may communicate the gestalt of the boat more meaningfully. This is certainly the case with a well-done caricature.

The artist can represent the boat in the way that she does because of a lifetime of visual experience with the world around

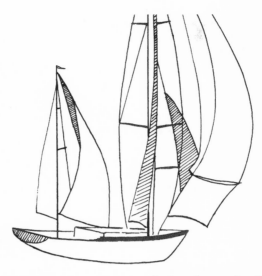

her and the things it contains, including boats. I will use the term *models* to describe the internal structures in which she organizes and stores that experience. She can picture a boat the way she does because her internal models of boats and their structure allow her to filter, select, and organize the necessary details into a meaningful picture.

It's a bit like the use of a police "identa-kit" to help a witness put together a composite picture. The kit contains a large number of different hairlines, noses, mouths, eyebrows, and other facial features. The operator of the kit presents the witness with various combinations, until a satisfactory likeness is obtained. The range of faces which can be constructed in this way is large enough to permit a recognizable likeness of almost anyone. The artist drawing the boat is working with a much larger set of potential picture elements, stored internally in her system of visual models. The basic process she goes through is much the same nonetheless.

Our ongoing sense of vision works in much the same way as do our other perceptual systems. We do not see objective images of the external world like those produced by a camera. Rather, we see interpretative images we construct by combining cues drawn from our visual flow with expectations and past experience drawn from our stored perceptual models. We see mostly what we expect to see, what we know how to see on the basis of our past experience.

This is strikingly illustrated by a set of experiments with visual perception carried out in the late 1940s. Subjects were asked to identify playing cards flashed before them for short controlled periods of time. The presentation interval was initially too short to allow recognition, but was gradually lengthened until reliable identification was possible. In addition to ordinary playing cards, the deck contained a few cards of the wrong color, e.g., a red six of spades. At short presentation intervals all cards were difficult to recognize, but as the interval was lengthened, subjects could identify increasing fractions of the cards. The anomalous cards were identified too, but as ordinary cards. A red six of spades, for example, would be seen as a six of hearts or a six of spades, depending on whether the subject used color or shape as the primary cue.

At slightly longer presentation intervals, subjects would make the same incorrect identification, but would begin to feel uncomfortable about it. They knew something was wrong, but could not put their finger on what it was. At still longer intervals, they would see something wrong with the card, but might see an anomaly quite different from the actual one. Some subjects saw purple hearts; others saw black spades with red fringe around the edges. When the intervals became long enough, they would see what was wrong and correctly identify the anomalous cards. After identifying several such cards, they could identify these correctly at much shorter presentation intervals. They now knew how to "see" red spades.

A few subjects would continue to identify anomalous cards incorrectly even after repeated exposures at long presentation intervals. The experimenters described this as a tendency on the part of those subjects to "fixate after receiving a minimum of confirmation."

This experiment provides a good metaphor for the role of perceptual models in perception more generally. Long experience has taught us that cards come in four suits—hearts, diamonds, clubs, and spades—and that the former two are red while the latter two are black. We have no categories for black hearts or red spades, making them much more difficult to see. The way subjects responded to these cards, therefore, is indicative of how we see things not adequately represented by our existing models.

If the thing goes by quickly, we may not notice it at all. We just see something we know how to see instead. As more evidence accumulates (longer presentation interval) we begin to become uncomfortable with that perception, and to look for an alternative. We may see the thing correctly, or we may construct something part way between our old misperception and the "objective truth." The purple hearts and the black spades with red fringes seen by some subjects illustrate this latter possibility.

When enough evidence has accumulated we can make the shift and see what has been there (red spades) all the time. Once we do, we can continue to see the thing with levels of evidence we would have earlier ignored. The amount of evidence required to make this shift will vary from person to person; a few people, once they have fixated on one perception, will continue to hold it in the face of what most would see as overwhelming contrary evidence.

In trying this experiment informally I found one friend who continued to see a six of hearts after I had handed him the card and he was holding it in his hand looking at it.

The same kind of thing can happen with all forms of perception, of course, even those based on apparently careful and explicit conscious reasoning. If the model through which the perception forms does not contain appropriate categories to allow recognition of an event, that event may be unrecognized or misinterpreted, even in the face of considerable evidence. How likely this is will depend in part on the kind and amount of attention given the evidence. On a personal level, such phenomena are the source of many misunderstandings, while on a national level, they are the stuff of which policy blunders and intelligence failures are made.

This experiment clearly demonstrates that we do not always see what we think we see—that the maxim "seeing is believing" is not necessarily true. We can fail to see what we do not expect; and we may see something which is not there at all. The subjects in the experiment did not just fail to see the red spade; they saw a black spade or a red heart in its place. Because they saw what they expected to see, they could not see the unexpected.

Another example of our ability to visually construct something that is not really there is given by the "subjective contours" in the "virtual triangle" shown below.

Most people can see the edges of the white triangle clearly, though those edges do not exist in any objective sense. We see scenes containing objects, not arbitrary visual patterns. We subjectively construct the white triangle because that triangle provides a natural explanation for the incompleteness of the black triangle and the circles. We interpret our visual input through a model of the external world as a place made of objects, often seen in such a way that one partially obscures another. The perception of a white triangle "on top" of the other "objects" in this scene is consistent with such a world model.

This filling-in of contours in order to see objects does not occur only with simple and regular geometric patterns. It is an integral part of our everyday seeing, which we fail to notice unless it is isolated and brought to our specific attention. Seeing is not the simple passive process we often imagine it to be—in which objective information about the outside world passes directly to a waiting mind. Rather, it is a highly active and interactive learned activity. The mind and brain combine new information collected by the senses with preexisting knowledge and belief to construct an ongoing image of the world being "seen" which is reasonably consistent with both the new information and the preexisting knowledge. You may "see" the same new information differently, depending on the preexisting knowledge you combine it with, as the B/13 and other ambiguous figures show.

Different people, coming from different visual backgrounds, may see very different things when presented with the same visual scene. Aspects of the scene which stand out clearly to one person may be almost invisible to another. When I stand on an urban street corner, I have no trouble finding the street sign, but I would have a great deal of trouble tracking an animal in the desert. An Australian aborigine, growing up in an environment where tracking was an important survival skill, could see the marks left by the animal without difficulty; but he might find it impossible to pick the street sign out of the visual welter of the urban scene.

We've been talking about perceptions of things we are conscious of as complete entities, like faces, 13's, or street signs, but the process repeats itself at much lower levels. Even the "building blocks" from which I construct my visual images— the little pieces I seldom notice as entities in themselves, like edges, corners, flat surfaces—come out of my past experience as reflected in my stored models of the visual world. As someone who grew up in a "carpentered" environment, most of the objects and structures I saw as I was learning to see were man-made, and regular in form. The building blocks from which I create my visual images thus probably contain a great many regular geometric shapes and figures—straight lines, corners, rectangles, and the like.

The aborigine, on the other hand, grows up in a natural environment which is far more varied and contains few of the regular geometric patterns found in mine. His perceptual models are organized around building blocks which are useful for representing features he needs to recognize in order to find water, track prey, and do other things necessary for his survival. What these building blocks are, I don't know, and I'm not sure we would have words for them in English. They would probably be as meaningless to me as the regularities of my environment apparent to me would be to him.

These very low level differences have been demonstrated in

comparisons of visual acuity between urban dwellers and
Canadian Cree Indians. Visual acuity refers to the sharpness of
vision, the ability to see detail. It is measured in terms of the
ability to distinguish a grid of alternating black and white
stripes. A coarse grid (wide stripes) will appear as stripes, while
a fine grid (narrow lines) will appear as a uniform grey. The point
at which a person is unable to distinguish between the grid and
a uniform grey is a measure of his or her acuity.

In urban populations, visual acuity is significantly higher
when the visual stimulus has a horizontal or vertical orientation
than when it has an oblique orientation. You and I, in other
words, see better when we look at something which is straight
up and down than when we look at something tilted at a 45°
angle. This is probably because the urban environments we
learned to see in are filled with vertical and horizontal contours
—walls, windows, doors, etc.—but contain relatively few
oblique contours. To experience this difference, move back
slowly from the book and see what happens to the two grids
below.

 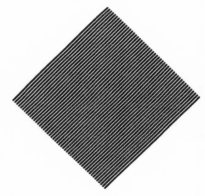

If you are like most people, the lines in the horizontal grid
will still be visible at the point where the oblique grid becomes
a grey blur. Studies of Canadian Cree Indians, on the other hand,
have shown a much more even acuity, independent of the
orientation of the stimulus. Their environment is much richer
in contours at all orientations, with even their dwellings having
curved doorways and ceilings.

It now seems clear that vision is not the direct, objective sense it appears to be. We see what we know how to see, and what we expect to see. From our visual experience we build internal models of the world and the things it contains, and we use those models to filter and interpret the stream of optical images which flows across our retinas. We find it easier to see things we are familiar with, and harder to see things which are outside our past visual experience. At low levels in our visual system this is reflected in our visual acuity, while at higher levels it is reflected in our failure to see red spades, or in the ease with which we can see subjective contours or shapes in the clouds drifting by.

THE OTHER SENSES

Our other senses operate in much the same way. We hear what we know how to hear, taste what we know how to taste, and even feel textures and temperatures as we know how to feel them. What we hear or taste depends very much on the context in which the sensation occurs, and on the expectations that context engenders. The roar of a jet plane and the roar of a waterfall are similar, and we may hear the same loud roar as either depending on where we are and which seems more reasonable in the circumstances. In a blindfolded taste test a piece of raw potato may be mistaken for an apple, even though the two taste very different when compared side by side. The mistake apparently comes about because the taster subconsciously uses texture clues rather than flavor.

We can understand spoken language across a broad range of speakers, accents, and conditions because we have well-developed auditory models of language against which to match incoming speech. But "red spades" also exist in speech. An individual word misspoken or slurred, or even an inappropriate word out of context, is likely to go completely unnoticed. The meaningless word "chack," carefully pronounced, will be heard as "chick" in a conversation about poultry and as "check" if the subject is banking. Even the reply, "Fine, I've just murdered my wife," to the conversational question "How's it going?" may elicit no particular reaction if given in the kind of polite, cheery voice which the questioner expects.

We can see these perceptual phenomena at work in controlled experimental situations because we (as "observers") can know the "true" situation, and can see how the subject's perception differs from that "truth." We know that the subjects shown red spades "saw" something else, for example, and that a fixed optical pattern like the faces/vase figure can be perceived in more than one way.

We don't see these same phenomena at work in more "natural" situations, because all we have to go on is our consensus perception of the situation. If everyone we come in contact with perceives a situation in the same way, we accept that perception as true, even though we may all be agreeing on the same misperception. We don't have the same kind of independent check on what's really "out there" that exists in the controlled experiment.

Think about a situation like the red spade experiment, but where the subjects could only talk to each other with no "experimenter" to explain anything. Imagine you had been through the experiment and had failed to see the red spades, and that the same was true of everyone you talked to. You would all agree on what you had seen, and there would be no way for you to find out that you had misperceived some red spades.

If one person did happen to see them, he would probably have a very hard time convincing anyone else of that fact. "But we didn't see them," the others would say, "and besides, everyone knows there's no such thing as a red spade." Against this strong consensus, he might begin to doubt his own perceptions, and decide in the end that *he* must have been mistaken. On the other hand, if the cards continue to flash by, and the one who thought he saw the red spade persists, he should be able to see it again. As he becomes more certain of what he has seen, he may succeed in pointing it out to others—by telling them what to look for, and perhaps when to look most carefully. Not everyone will see it, nor even believe it when they do. But some will, and those who do may gain a better understanding of the world they live in.

I now want to try to show you a tactile "red spade," a trick our perceptions play which we all accept as reality. By "all" here, I mean the vast majority of the human race, all but a few highly exceptional individuals such as the few genuine masters in the "soft" internal martial arts. I happened across this in the course of trying to understand some of the exceptional capabilities attributed to those masters. The exercise below and others which follow, will allow you to directly experience some of the concepts this book is about. This is an important adjunct to the intellectual understanding you get from reading and should not be ignored. Spend a little time with the exercise and give yourself the chance to have that experience.

Hold your right hand in front of you, and with your left hand grasp your right wrist from above, as shown. Now try to raise your right hand, at the same time you hold it in place with your left. Do that long enough and hard enough that you can really feel you're working at it, and notice the feeling of pushing that occurs in your wrists, arms and shoulders. Notice also that your attention focuses primarily on the point of contact between your left hand and right wrist, and that most of the energy from both hands seems to be directed into that point.

Now let's analyze what happened. You felt like you were pushing up hard with the right hand, and down hard with the left. The two pushes were equally strong, so they canceled each other out. That's why you felt stuck, and why no movement occurred. Right? Of course. And there are four suits of cards, and the spades are always black.

Try the same thing again. Get stuck the same way. Now shift

your attention away from the point of contact at the wrist and into
the muscles of your right arm and shoulder. Be aware of those
muscles and feel what they are doing. Concentrate very hard on
keeping them as they are. Without changing anything in your
right arm, release your hold and withdraw your left arm. See what
happens to your right arm.

Did your right arm pop up as a result of the restraining force
being removed, or did it stay essentially where it was, still stuck,
but with nothing holding it down? The first alternative is the
expected one, the one our consensus view of the world says
should happen. The second is what *does* happen if you really
follow the directions—if you don't change what you are doing in
your right arm as the left one is removed. I'm going to assume
now that the exercise worked for you and discuss what
happened. After that I'll talk about what you might have been
doing if it didn't work and suggest some ways you might try it
differently.

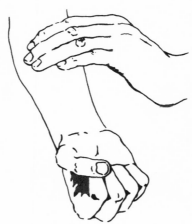

If you take your left hand away without changing what you are
doing in the right arm, the arm may raise slightly but it won't
move very far. It will remain rigidly stuck in space in approximately the position where it was restrained. You can still pump
energy into the hand, still push as hard as you were when you
were holding yourself down, but all that energy will just go into
making your arm rigid.

That's the same energy you thought was pushing up, against the restraining left hand. But it wasn't really. Most of your effort was going into holding the right hand rigid in space while you felt that the left hand was holding it down. At the same time, you were holding the left hand rigid in space while perceiving it pushing down against an upward pushing right hand.

All you really get from the grasp is a tactile sensation on your wrist. In response to that sensation, you make yourself rigid and interpret that rigidity as coming from outside, from the restraining hand. You push hard against yourself to increase your rigidity and blame the restraint for not letting you move. You create a tactile image of a stiff and rigid external world to explain the tactile sensation of the grasp on your wrist in the same way you create a visual image of a white triangle to explain the optical pattern we looked at earlier. In this way you create your own reality.

The implications of this sort of exercise, when you begin to really think about them, can be mindblowing. At least they were for me, at first. Those homilies like "all conflict is within you," or "you create your own limitations," which used to seem only symbolic suddenly take on new substance. Still, questions arise. What's really happening? If it is not really the apparent restraint that's keeping you from moving, could you decide to move anyway? How? I don't have complete answers for these questions, and I'm not sure complete answers exist. Their absence, in fact, is part of what makes the world an interesting place to live. I will give you some partial answers as the book develops. For the time being, though, I just want to address a couple of points briefly before going on to some other issues.

If you really are keeping yourself stuck, then it follows that you should also be able to move. To do that you just forget that you're stuck. In practice that's very difficult, because it goes against a lifetime of conditioning; but it can be done. Some people do it spontaneously in periods of extreme stress, like the twelve-year-old who lifted the car off his father. Others, like the T'ai Chi master who can toss someone across the room with a flick of his wrist, break down past conditioning and learn to function differently through long and disciplined practice and training. Whether or not you ever actually do that, you gain something from understanding that it can be done. That knowledge gives you a clearer picture of yourself and of the world you live in.

What normally happens in a physical interaction with another person, in which each of you thinks you feel the mass and strength of the other, is that both are acting in the same way. Each of you puts a lot of energy into being stuck and rigid, and attributes that stuckness to the other person. To feel stuck takes cooperation; you both have to work at it. That's what Carlos Castaneda's mentor don Juan means when he says that what we experience as reality is membership in an agreement, in which we cooperate with others to maintain our consensus. If we all agree to react the same way, we can all maintain our consensus reality quite well and nobody will be bothered by any "red spades." The thing which makes the T'ai Chi master appear so powerful is that he doesn't play by the same rules. Rather, he uses those rules against his opponent to the opponent's disadvantage.

If the exercise didn't work for you, if your right arm moved up when you took your left hand away, then you allowed what was happening in your right arm to change as you took your left hand away. To make the exercise work, you must become conscious of that change and inhibit it. I'll give you some suggestions on how to do that. If the exercise did work for you, you might want to skip over this discussion and go on to the beginning of the next section.

Get stuck again, with your left hand holding your right arm. Notice your attention, and where it is focused—probably on the point of contact between hand and wrist. Now watch what happens as you begin to take your left hand away. Your right arm moves to maintain the point of contact. Get stuck again. Begin to remove the left hand again in the same way, but now put your attention on your right arm, shoulder, and elbow. Notice that they are changing, that you are doing something different with them in order to maintain the contact between hand and wrist.

The change is subtle and hard to characterize well in words. It may be difficult to see at first, but it's there and you can find it. It comes just as you begin to take your left hand away, as the right arm begins to move. That's the change you have to inhibit in order to keep doing what you were doing while you held your wrist. Go back and try again to inhibit that change, and see what happens to your right arm when you take the left away. If you still have trouble, don't despair. Like catching a red spade for the first time, this can be hard. The medium I'm using to give you instructions, the printed page, is a poor one for this sort of thing. Personal contact and direct instruction work much better. If you haven't gotten it, show the instructions to a friend and let her try it. If you can find someone else who can do it, you can see it happening, and maybe she can help you with it.

INTELLECTUAL PERCEPTION

The examples we've looked at so far have all involved sense perception. Similar phenomena occur in our conceptual understanding of the world as well. One example of this concerns an observation my son made when he was about two years old. I was flying across the country frequently on business, usually for several days at a time. Both my children enjoyed the hustle of the airport, so they went often to see me off when I left and meet me when I returned. My wife told me that one time two or three days after I left, our son had been playing in the yard when an airliner passed overhead. He stopped playing and with the sudden grin of discovery pointed at the plane and exclaimed, "There's Daddy!"

My reaction when my wife told me about the incident was one of amusement. It was another of those funny things a child says. Then I began to think about what was involved; I realized that it had been a significant feat of inference, considering the knowledge available to him at the time. A two-year-old's world is a limited one. It consists of places he has actually experienced, with some fuzzy ideas about places he has been told about or heard of in stories. He does not yet have a very consistent picture of the area where he lives, let alone of a larger entity like a city. The concepts of a country the size of the United States, of cities at opposite sides of that country, and airplanes traveling between them, are completely beyond his experience.

What does he see, then, on his trips to the airport? He sees Daddy go onto a plane, and he sees the plane go up into the sky. Several days later he goes to the airport again to watch a plane come down from the sky and Daddy get off. He can't tell that it is a different plane from the first one. The inference that Daddy spent the week up in the sky, then, seems quite reasonable in light of what he knows. So does the inference, when he spots a plane while Daddy is gone, that it is the one Daddy is in. (I thought about this incident later, by the way, when I found that experts in child development believe that the ability to draw logical inferences doesn't develop until around age eight.)

The next example I want to look at concerns the same basic elements of misperception based on limited understanding, this time as seen by a culture rather than a single small boy. It involves religions known as "cargo cults" which grew out of the contact between Western technological society and the Pacific island cultures. These contacts began with the voyages of European explorers in the sixteenth century and grew steadily as time progressed. The nature of the contact changed dramatically during World War II. As the war against Japan progressed, American forces moved steadily across the Pacific. Each new island occupied became the staging base for the next assault. Large quantities of supplies of all types—food, clothing, ammunition, fuel—would be shipped in and stored until needed, sometimes forming small mountains of material along the beaches.

This activity imposed considerable shock on the native cultures. Where did all the "cargo" come from? These people saw the world as a collection of small islands in a world of water. They had no concept of a continental land mass, let alone the kind of urban-industrial society which could produce the mountains of goods confronting them. But such phenomena cannot go unexplained. If the true explanation is not within the grasp of the people involved, they will produce one which is. The result in this case was the "cargo cults," native religions which grew up to explain its origins and to provide their members with ways to obtain it for themselves. The cargo itself was seen as a gift from the gods who sent it to the white men in large metal canoes, or sometimes in great metal birds. The white men received it because they knew the proper spells and incantations. Indeed, they could often be seen talking into sticks (radios) praying for it, and making magical marks and performing other exotic rituals (doing paperwork). Thus, the cults believed, if only they could learn the secrets of these rituals, the gods would reward them richly with "cargo."

Some of the cult members also observed that the giant birds liked to land where their friends were. In order to lure them down, they constructed elaborate mock airstrips—cleared strips lined with mock aircraft made from wood and bamboo. Sometimes at night these strips were lined with torches to simulate landing lights. Conceptually, the idea is very similar to the use of decoys by duck hunters. It might even have worked sometime. Imagine a pilot, lost and running out of fuel, coming upon one of these strips and using it as an emergency field. How must he have felt to find himself a "gift of the gods," in answer to the prayers of the faithful?

Viewed from "enlightened" Western eyes, such cults appear as the height of primitive superstition and may seem almost laughable. If we take a less ethnocentric view, however, we can see the cults as the result of a natural attempt to explain a new phenomenon within an existing world-view. The use of the decoy airfields and attempts to duplicate the "rituals" from which the white men obtained the cargo were attempts to replicate the results of a poorly understood process by replicating the external artifacts accompanying that process. This is a common way of dealing with the world, one we all employ more often than we realize.

An example much closer to home, though still analogous in many ways to the cargo cults, is the contemporary "cult of systems analysis"—based on the belief that quantitative computer analyses using mathematical models will automatically provide good guidance in dealing with pressing human problems, particularly those arising in the administration of government.°

The cult of systems analysis still plays a significant role in

---

°My use of the term *systems analysis* is intended to be a broad one, encompassing activities with labels like "cost/benefit analysis," "econometrics," "operations analysis," and "policy analysis" as well as those labeled "systems analysis" per se. The distinctions made between these activities are sometimes useful from a highly technical perspective, but for present purposes are irrelevant.

contemporary American government, though not quite as much as during its heyday under Secretary of Defense Robert McNamara. Like the cargo cults, it owes much to a misunderstanding of activity started during World War II, though of course to a different kind of activity. In this case, the activity was that of British and American operations analysts in bringing their skills to bear on the problems of fighting a war. Using mathematical techniques, these analysts gained new insights into important military problems such as the deployment of antisubmarine warfare forces, and in some cases significantly affected the outcomes of military engagements.

Following the war, these same types of people continued to apply their talents to military (and later to civilian) problems at places like the Rand Corporation. They sometimes produced highly useful results, as the methods they employed could be extremely powerful aids to human judgment. Because the activity seemed successful, it prospered, and the numbers of people doing it multiplied. The development of the digital computer made it feasible to tackle larger and larger problems and created a kind of superhuman mystique. Many of these people came to see the models and the techniques applied, rather than the human intellect applying them, as the primary source of whatever knowledge resulted. The focus of the activity shifted increasingly toward the mindless application of computational techniques.

A strong parallel can be seen with the cargo cults. Systems analysis, as the use of mathematical models and techniques to *assist* competent and informed human judgment, can be of considerable value. Many of the people who currently engage in it, however, have no more understanding of the nature of human judgment and intuition than the island cultures had of urban-industrial society. The contemporary systems analyst attempts to produce knowledge through mechanically emulating the computational methods which he believes were the basis of successful systems analysis in the past. But like the cargo cultist, he is simply attempting to reproduce the external artifacts which accompany, but do not themselves produce, the phenomenon he seeks.

THE PERCEPTUAL PROCESS PARADIGM

The same thread runs through all these examples, from the faces/vase and the red spades to the cargo cults and systems analysis. The preceiver in each case (whether my son, the cargo cultist, the subject in the red spades experiment or the systems analyst) sees only part of what is before him—the part consistent with and reinforcing his prior experience and expectations.

My intent is not to disparage this form of perception, even though it has led to wrong conclusions in most of the examples discussed thus far. It serves us well most of the time. The examples have been, for the most part, the pathological exceptions. Only by looking at these exceptions, however, can we see how the basic mechanism works and what its strengths and limitations might be in everyday usage. Then we can begin to understand what it really shows us of the world around us. The core elements common to these various examples, and to others we'll meet later, can be described as follows. A *perceiver* creates an *image* of the thing he or she perceives. This image is constructed in part from the new information being received from the environment and in part from expectation and past experience.

The perceiver does not see the thing itself, or even the pattern of information which he is currently receiving. The stream of information being received from the environment we will call *perceptual flow,* and use the term *model* in a general sense to refer to representations of external phenomena which people make and use in various ways. We can then describe what the perceiver sees as an internal *model* of the thing being perceived, produced from a combination of *cues* from that perceptual flow and elements drawn from preexisting *perceptual models.* Those models serve to screen and filter the perceptual flow and also to interpret what passes through that filter. At the same time, the models themselves are changed by the process so that the expectations brought to each new moment of perception are not quite the same as the moment before. Often the change seems minor, perhaps even negligible. At times, though, it can be highly significant, as when the perceiver sees a red spade for the first time.

In basic concept, this model of perception is not particularly new or original. Variations of it are common in the literature of cognitive psychology. The description of perception given by Ulric Neisser, for example, in *Cognition and Reality* is very similar if we equate my concept of "model" with his concept of "schema." It can also be found in various forms in the philosophical and esoteric literature, including Plato's cave, the Eastern idea that the sensible world is an illusion, and don Juan's description of perceived reality as an "agreement." It is also present in the philosophy of science, in Thomas Kuhn's account of the nature of scientific revolution.

What I hope to provide here is an integrating perspective on the common structure underlying all the concepts mentioned above, and on the wide variety of different processes to which they each apply. I do not intend that this model, to which I will refer as the *perceptual process paradigm*, be taken as a rigorous scientific model whose elements (models, cues, images, etc.) can be given precise definitions and can be unambiguously identified in particular situations. Rather, it should be thought of as a loose description of a common underlying structure, a metaphor for thinking about the commonalities of such diverse processes as vision and science, language and religion (all of which will be discussed as we proceed).

2

Language as a Perceptual Process

Language itself is a perceptual process, with all the characteristics discussed in the last chapter. We create verbal images of
the world around us, and those images form a significant part
of our perception of that world. These verbal images are *not*
objective descriptions of the things they describe. Rather, they
reflect a mixture of the actual characteristics of the thing itself
and of the preconceptions and expectations created by our past
experience, as well as by the structure of the language within
which we think.

We use language to organize and think about the world we
live in. We make verbal images of our immediate surroundings
("the rug is red; the walls are white"), as well as of things far
removed from us in space and time ("Paris is a city in France;
Columbus discovered America in 1492"). We use language to
describe characteristics and relationships which we think of as
objective attributes of the objects to which they attach (heavier
than, red, wooden) as well as characteristics which reflect the
subjective judgment of the perceiver (nicer than, worthwhile,
ugly). We combine, modify and manipulate those images in
order to better understand the world around us and to predict

the results of our actions in it. And in all these activities, language serves as the medium through which our perception and understanding takes place.

We use verbal models (i.e., models made up of words and verbal categories) as filters through which we perceive and interpret much of our experience. Some people, for example, see all politicians as being either "liberal" or "conservative," admitting no other gradations. They react to a particular politician by placing him in one of the categories and judging him accordingly. If he doesn't really fit either category, they shove him into one or the other anyway, perhaps feeling somewhat uncomfortable about it without really knowing why. This behavior, you will notice, is much like that of the subject who has no existing conceptual category within which to place the red spade. There are many people, including those who pride themselves on being "hardnosed," "realistic" or "scientific," who see the world only in terms of things which can be unambiguously characterized in precise verbal terms— things which can be measured, labeled and quantified. These people perceive the world only in terms of their verbal models, admitting the reality of only those things which their models describe.

There is an important difference between language and the sensory perceptual processes such as vision. The images we produce with the sensory processes are private, belonging to each of us individually, while we can make our verbal images public and share them with others. Language, then, is a medium for communication as well as perception. Communication, ultimately, is a sharing of perception. In writing this book, for example, I am trying to share my models of how the world works and how we perceive it. I do this by providing you with cues which I hope you will interpret through your perceptual models in a manner which will allow you to understand mine. If I am successful, you will be able to modify your perceptual models in ways that will eventually make them more like mine. I will pay less attention here to the communicative aspects of language than to the perceptual, but I do want to note that they exist and play an important role in the nature of language and in our use of it.

At a quite general level, language itself can be thought of as a perceptual model through which we filter and interpret the ongoing flow of our experience. Our language defines the things we can recognize and the relationships between them which we can perceive and understand. The cues we select to form our perceptual images, then, are the aspects of our experience which we bother to notice and name, and the images thus produced are the verbal descriptions which fill up the word stream that flows through our heads.

Things for which we have words are much easier to think about than things for which we do not, and things with separate names are easier to think about as distinct than are things for which we use the same word. Indeed, some people find it difficult even to conceive of aspects of experience for which there are no words to describe. But the set of things for which there are words is not the same in all languages, leading people who think in different languages to divide the world into very different sets of "things."

The Chinese use different words to describe rice in various forms and at different stages of development—growing in the paddy, threshed but not yet milled, milled but uncooked, or cooked and ready to eat. There is no Chinese equivalent to the English word "rice"—no single word which describes the plant as well as the grain in any of its forms or stages of development. The closest Chinese equivalent of the English *rice* means *"cooked rice ready to eat,"* but that word also has a meaning similar to the generic word *food* in English. The Chinese equivalent of "Have you eaten?" would literally translate as "Have you had your rice?"

To take another example, Eskimos use different words for, and thus see as basically different, things which we would see as different forms of the same basic entity "snow"—falling snow, slushy snow, wind-driven snow, etc. The Aztecs, on the other hand, make fewer distinctions in this area than we do, using different forms of the same basic word for "cold," "ice," and "snow." "Ice" is the noun form, "cold" the adjectival, and "snow" translates as "ice mist." In the Hopi Indian language, a single word means "all flying things except birds." This one Hopi term, then, would apply equally to an airplane, a pilot, an airline passenger, a mosquito, or a butterfly.°

This doesn't mean, of course, that a Hopi can't distinguish between a butterfly and an airline passenger, or that you and I can't distinguish in English between various kinds of snow. We can make those distinctions using combinations of context, adjectival modifiers and the like. But the very nature of the distinction is different in different languages. We see different kinds of snow as variants of the same basic entity—snow—while the Eskimo sees different entities, though related. We see the airline passenger and the butterfly as clearly different entities, having very little in common, while the Hopi sees them as variants of the same basic "thing which flies but is not a bird." Our distinctions appear to us as the natural and obvious ones because they are the ones we have grown up with and become accustomed to. They are no more natural in any absolute sense, however, than any others.

Any language makes those distinctions which users of the language find necessary or useful. The distinctions made by different nouns are generally more basic and important than the distinctions made by adjectives or other modifiers. Different forms of snow play a more important role in Eskimo life than in our lives, hence the need for natural and continuing distinction between them. Snow and cold have little meaning to the Aztecs, on the other hand, so that they need even fewer degrees of distinction than we do.

This same phenomenon operates even within a single language and is a major source of much of the specialized jargon we find so senseless when others use it. Specialists concerned with a narrow field of interest will need to make sharper distinctions within that field than will nonspecialists. Thus botanists develop elaborate jargon to describe what most people think of as "weeds," and anthropologists create complex

---

°This and other examples in this chapter relating to American Indian language are drawn from *Language, Thought, and Reality; Selected Writings of Benjamin Lee Whorf.* Whorf, a linguist who died in 1941, wrote extensively on the relationship between thought and language. The position I take here, that language plays a very influential role in perception, is sometimes referred to as the "Whorfian hypothesis."

terminology to differentiate between systems of kinship and social organization most of us have never encountered and wouldn't be much interested in if we did. The use of a single word in one language to cover a range of meanings requiring many words in another language is the most obvious way the language we use affects the way we think. But there are subtler and perhaps more important effects. The basic structure of a language—the *kinds* of word-categories it uses and the *relationships* it admits between those categories—has a major influence on the way users of that language organize their perceptions of reality, and on what they see as "objective" characteristics of the external world.

In English, as in most European languages, the two principal word-categories are *nouns* describing objects and *verbs* describing actions involving those objects. The principal relationships described by English are of the "object-does-action-to-object" (subject-verb-object) variety. Thinking in English, we perceive a world made up primarily of objects—people, trees, chairs, stones—and we perceive actions as being done by and to those objects. We assign an artificial, object-like character to aspects of reality which aren't really objects at all, at least in any material sense, such as day, summer, thunder, a handwave. When we need to express an idea of action in which no object participates as subject, we create a fictitious subject in order to retain the subject-verb structure of description, as in *"it* is raining." We do this naturally, without conscious thought or effort. That is the way we have learned to think, because that is the way the language we think in structures the world. It is so natural and effortless that we assume those word-categories and relationships reflect self-evident objective characteristics of reality which all people (indeed, perhaps, all conscious beings) everywhere would experience in the same way.

But it isn't really that way at all. Some languages are structured around quite different basic word-categories and relationships. They project very different pictures of the basic nature of reality as a result. The language of the Nootka Indians in the Pacific Northwest, for example, has only one principal word-category; it denotes happenings or events. A verbal form like "eventing" might better describe this word category, except that such a form doesn't sound right in English, with its emphasis on noun forms. We might think of Nootka as composed entirely of verbs, except that they take no subjects or objects as English verbs do. The Nootka, then, perceive the world as a stream of transient events, rather than as the collection of more or less permanent objects which we see. Even something which we see clearly as a physical object, like a house, the Nootka perceive of as a long-lived temporal event. The literal English translation of the Nootka concept might be something like "housing occurs," or "it houses."

The Hopi language has both verbs and nouns, but uses them in ways different from us. Events (described by verbs) rather than objects (described by nouns) are the principal conceptual entities making up the world. Events occur in their own right, rather than as actions performed by objects (as is the case for verbs in English). Nouns describe objects, but only real objects which have a degree of persistance or duration. "Storm" or "cloud" are about the lower limit for nouns in Hopi. Briefer phenomena, such as lightning, smoke, or a wave of the hand are thought of as events and described by verbs. Verbs may stand alone and need not be given fictitious noun subjects as in English. Thus a Hopi might say simply "raining" rather than "it is raining;" or "flashing" rather than "a light is flashing;" or even "running" rather than "he is running" or "see him run," simply calling attention to the action and treating the actor as a self-evident part of that action.

All language must express ideas of tendency, duration and intensity. English expresses these ideas with concepts and metaphors drawn from our perceptions of material objects in physical space. We express duration with terms like *long, short* and *much.* We describe tendency with terms like *grow, turn* and *approach.* We use *heavy, low* and *large* to express intensity. We use spatial metaphors for all sorts of nonspatial ideas—we *grasp* an idea or concept, or *reach* an understanding or a compromise. Through these metaphors we see abstract non-material aspects of reality in the same way we see the concrete and material aspects—as consisting basically of objects which perform action on one another, and are otherwise similar to material objects in physical space.

Yet such ideas are not inherently spatial and need not be conceptualized in spatial terms. Hopi does not characterize them that way at all but expresses them in ways that bear no relationship to spatial concepts. One relatively minor way in which this difference might manifest itself is in the Hopi tendency to gesture much less than we do when talking. Whorf suggests that this might be due to the fact that much of our gesturing serves to illustrate and reinforce spatial metaphors for nonspatial concepts. We reach out into the air as we speak of "grasping" for an idea, and we separate our hands to show how "far apart" two points of view might be. Hopi ways of expressing these ideas are nonspatial so they have no way, or need, to strengthen them with gestures.

We see time as a kind of "stuff" flowing steadily past at a uniform rate. It can be measured, divided up into uniform increments, bought, sold, saved and used in various ways. It seems as if we perceive it this way because this is the way it is, objectively, and no reasonable person could possibly perceive it otherwise. Yet the Hopi apparently perceive it otherwise! They have no terms for time as we know it. They have concepts of change and duration, of course, of one event flowing after another and of a general growing later and later. But there is no "time," no stuff or thing which can be expressed by a noun, measured and cut up into pieces.

Units of time, like days, are objects in English; they can be grouped and counted like objects. We say "five days" in the same way we say "five men," and see the two constructions as parallel. In Hopi, however, that parallelism does not exist. Five men can be experienced; they can be brought togther as a group in one place. But days can be experienced only one at a time as they occur, and not in a group.

Besides, they are not separate entities at all, the way people are. They are cyclic phases in the process of growing later, described not by nouns but by something we might classify as a kind of adverb. The passage of these phases is expressed by an ordinal counting of them as they occur, but not by the unthinkable (in Hopi) artifice of pretending to experience several in a group. Thus a Hopi might say "on the fifth daying," or "after the fourth daying has passed," but never "five days."

The perceptual concepts which languages like Nootka and Hopi embody, and the images of the world which those concepts produce, may seem artificial and even bizarre to us—inadequate vehicles for characterizing the world as we see it. But that strangeness results from our lack of experience with those concepts, and the appearance of inadequacy reflects our particular ethnocentric biases. The richness and differentiation of description provided by such languages is as great as that provided by English, neither better nor worse in any absolute sense—only different. But because such languages differentiate the world in different terms, the world will appear different, and indeed may be a very different place to people who think in those terms.

The subject-verb-object structure of English encourages us to think in terms of A does B to C. We see the world in terms of sharp causes and effects, the former preceding the latter. Ideas of cause and effect as the basic mechanism that makes things work are so deeply embodied in Western thought and language that it seems difficult to think of any other kind of relationship as playing a significant role in the way the universe behaves.

Yet there are other possibilities, however alien they might at first seem. One such is what Carl Jung calls *synchronicity,* the idea that apparently unconnected events occurring at the same time may be related in an acausal way, taking place concurrently because they are all part of the same total pattern of the condition of the universe at that moment. English has no good way of expressing such a relationship, and perhaps that is part of the reason it seems so alien and difficult. It is more easily expressed in Hopi and some of the Oriental languages which have different grammatical structures. It is also a principle which plays an important role in Oriental thought.

The structure of our language can also influence the relationship we feel with what we write or say. The use of passive, impersonal constructions, such as "it can be shown," or "the data imply" is common in scientific, technical or bureaucratic writing. Such constructions separate the writer from the writing, allowing him to feel little or no *personal* involvement with what he says. In scientific writing, this reflects the perception that knowledge exists apart from knower, that the scientist is simply a detached objective observer who uncovers and records what already exists. In nonscientific areas such as bureaucratic writing, and in pseudo-scientific endeavors such as systems analysis, it provides the writer a sense of detachment which allows him to avoid *personal* responsibility for what he writes. After all, it's not his fault that "the data imply..." or "the study shows..." The systems analyst or bureaucrat can thus separate his personal and professional feelings. When his job demands it, he can easily advocate or argue for positions which he would personally find unsupportable if he really thought about them.

This is, perhaps, the same sense of disinterest in one's work which Robert Pirsig, in his essay on *Zen and the Art of Motorcycle Maintenance,* identifies as a pervasive and destructive characteristic of contemporary American society. He sees it as part of the way that technology is now viewed and applied; he also identifies the impersonality of technical writing and the lack of involvement which it fosters/reflects as symptomatic of the larger attitude.

Language is a filter through which our perception of the world around us passes—a lens which shapes and distorts our images of the reality we inhabit. It brings some aspects of that reality into sharp focus, while blurring others so that we barely notice them. This happens so naturally that we are hardly aware of the process, at least as long as we only think about the world through a single language, like English, or through a group of closely related languages which all structure reality in much the same way, like the modern European languages. Only by looking at a very different language, like Hopi, can we begin to get some idea, however inadequate, of the influence language has on our perception of the world. The role language plays in perception is perhaps analogous to the role context plays (reading across or reading up and down) in perceiving the ambiguous B/13 shown earlier. Just as the context in which we see the figure will subtly influence the way we see it, so does the language we use to symbolize and describe the world subtly (or perhaps not so subtly) influence the way we see and understand that world.

Yet in spite of the very considerable differences in perception produced by differences in the structure of various languages, all human beings still share the same basic perceptual processes. They see the world with their vision, touch and handle solid objects, etc., and they characterize these experiences, to themselves as well as to others, by linear strings of verbal symbols or written equivalents thereof. These strong commonalities of process produce similarities in the resulting perceptions of the world. These similarities are strong enough to make it possible to find equivalencies between very different languages, and so to translate between one and another. It is only because translation is possible, in fact, that we can see how different languages can be.

How might things look to beings without language—and with basic perceptual processes structured along very different lines from ours? At first thought, it might seem that such creatures must necessarily see the world in much simpler terms than we do, must necessarily be of limited intelligence like the "lower" animals with whom we share the world. Human thought is so inexorably tied up with our use of language that we tend to see language and thought as almost synonymous. It seems as if language is necessary for thought, at least for the kinds of complex abstract thought we associate with the term "intelligence."

That may not be the case, however. We can certainly describe intelligence without tying it to language—as the ability to create, use and communicate complex ideas and characterizations of the world, perhaps. We humans use language to accomplish these ends, to be sure. But there is no reason, in principle, why other creatures might not be able to create, use and communicate equally complex concepts and ideas through a totally non-linguistic medium.

It's possible, in fact, that we share this planet with such creatures right now, the cetaceans (dolphins and whales) who live throughout the world's oceans. The evidence (both anatomical and behavioral) for high cetacean intelligence is strong, and it seems plausible that their capabilities for thought and communication match or exceed ours in richness and complexity, but use nothing remotely resembling the sequential strings of symbols we call language. To explore this possibility we must begin by looking at the differences between the human and cetacean environments and the perceptual mechanisms each has evolved to deal with those environments.

We humans live on the surface of the planet, in a transparent medium (air) in which we can see a long way. We have a highly developed sense of vision from which we get much of our information about the external world. Most things are opaque to visible light, so that we see the world as made up of solid objects with well defined boundaries. We recognize things by the way they look, so that a stuffed animal may appear indistinguishable from a live animal until we have watched it long enough to be sure that it isn't moving.

Hearing plays a distinctly secondary role for us, and we use it quite differently. We hear sounds produced by our surroundings —voices, footsteps, the wind, machinery operating. All sound results from movement or other activity on the part of the thing producing the sound, so we think of sound as something a creature or thing *does or makes,* in contrast with visual appearance, which is something a thing intrinsically *has.* All of this seems so obvious as to hardly be worth spelling out in this kind of detail. But it is not the only possible way things could be; it is only the result of our particular set of circumstances.

Dolphins live in a very different environment, and perceive it very differently.° The sea is often murky, growing darker with increasing depth. Vision is a less useful sense underwater than on the surface, and underwater creatures use it less than we do. The dolphins' primary sense is acoustic. But unlike our passive sense of hearing, theirs is an active sense in that the dolphin sends sound out into his environment and then perceives his surroundings on the basis of the echoes which come back. The best visual analogy, perhaps, would be to suppose we lived in a naturally dark world and carried around our own built-in floodlights.

That analogy is far from exact, however, because of differences between light and sound as illumination sources. Most things we look at are opaque to light, to take one example,

---

°Much of the specific information I will be discussing derives from studies of the bottlenosed dolphin (Tursiops truncatus), a highly intelligent species which has been studied extensively in captivity. The overall principles, though, apply to cetaceans generally.

while many things of interest to the dolphin (such as fish or other dolphins) are at least partially transparent to sound. Instead of the kind of surface image we are used to, the dolphin probably "sees" things in three dimensions. To a dolphin, then, a statue of a dolphin would appear quite different from a real dolphin, even though they might look identical to us.

We perceive different wavelengths of light as different colors, and we think of color as an attribute of the object reflecting the light. Dolphins may not perceive anything like color acoustically, and they probably use acoustical wavelength differences quite differently. The smallest object which can be distinguished (with either light or sound) approximates the wavelength of the illumination. The wavelengths of visible light are on the order of a millionth of an inch, so play no role in ordinary vision. The acoustic wavelengths used by dolphins range from a few feet to fractions of an inch, however, so that an object may "look" quite different, depending on the wavelength used to view it. Dolphins seem to utilize low-frequency scans to get a coarse overall picture of the environment, and shift to higher frequencies to examine things in more detail.

Dolphins emit different kinds of sound patterns in their echo-locating, getting different information back as a result. Let's look at one particular type of pattern and the information that a dolphin might receive from it. Remember that this is only one of many patterns which dolphins use, so their perception of their environment is undoubtedly more varied and complex than outlined here.

As dolphins move around, they often emit a sound pattern whose frequency or pitch rises linearly with time. The graph of this pattern has the visual appearance of a slash mark (/) and for this reason John Lilly has labeled it a "slash call." The slash call may range from 5KHZ (five thousand cycles per second) to 15KHZ or higher, and may last from one-tenth to six-tenths of a second. Dolphins placed in an unfamiliar environment (such as a new oceanarium tank) often swim around emitting slash calls for awhile, apparently exploring their new surroundings. As they become familiar with the area, their echo-locating decreases.

The speed of sound in sea water is approximately 5000 feet

per second, so the leading edge of a slash call lasting one half second will travel 2500 feet before the call ends. The echo of an object 500 feet away will return while the last three-fifths of the slash call is still going out, and the outgoing call will interfere with the returning echo. The dolphin will hear what is known as the "beat frequency" difference between the two interfering signals. (You may have experienced this phenomenon when tuning a musical instrument. If the instrument is slightly out of tune with the standard against which it is compared, the difference can be heard as a regular beat.) The shape of the slash call is such that the beat-frequency difference will depend only on the distance between the dolphin and the object returning the echo. If the dolphin and object are both motionless, the beat frequency will remain constant, while if the dolphin is closing on the object, the beat frequency will fall.

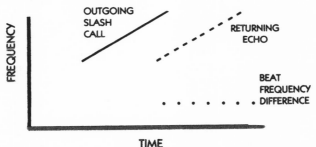

The dolphin can determine direction stereophonically and distance and relative motion from the beat frequency. The slash call and its echo, then, provide a low resolution image of the dolphin's environment. This image will be quite different from the visual images we see, but it is probably as meaningful to the dolphin as our visual images are to us. Pretend now that you are a dolphin, and imagine what that image might be like. I'll describe it visually, using color as a proxy for frequency. Red corresponds to a low frequency return, and the frequency increases as we move up the spectrum toward violet.

Imagine yourself floating still in the water, sending out slash calls to map your surrounding. What you get back, in our terms, is a pattern of colors. Nearby objects appear red, while farther away things appear yellow, green, blue and eventually violet. A fish or another dolphin moving toward you gradually changes color as it moves, shifting from violet through yellow and toward red. You see it not as a single opaque surface, but as a pulsating translucent mass.

Now you begin moving. As you do everything changes color, with things shifting toward red as you approach them and toward violet as they recede into the distance. You control the relationship between color and distance by the way you shape your slash call, and you extend or reduce the range of the image as your needs change. To examine something more closely you can give up the slash call altogether and shift to a different kind of pattern. The image then dissolves and a new one, very different in form, takes its place.

The processing all this requires—sorting returning echoes by direction, interpreting beat frequencies, etc.—seems awfully complicated, and you might wonder whether the dolphin could really create a usable image in this way. But dolphins probably don't really require any more complex processing to produce their acoustic images than we do to create the visual images we see on a continuing basis, never giving it a second thought.

Now let's shift from perception to communication, and see what these differences between cetacean and human perception imply about communication and language. First we must decide what we mean by *language*—what the term encompasses and what it excludes. *Language,* in my view, involves the use of sequential strings of symbols to represent ideas and aspects of the world of interest to the users of the language. Words are the symbols used by ordinary spoken language, and we combine those words into phrases, sentences, and larger units to produce more complex meaning structures. This definition encompasses many forms of human communication but not all. It covers spoken and written natural language, computer languages and "sign language." It excludes "body language," touch communication between lovers, and still or moving pictures. Not everyone will agree, but this provides a useful working definition for present purposes.

Human language evolved to serve two basic functions—communication and reasoning. We also use language to record and preserve information, but that was unimportant from an evolutionary point of view. Language of the complexity we use today requires a highly developed intellect, and it seems likely that the intellect and the language evolved concurrently, each aiding and supporting the other. Language may have begun with the use of sounds to claim territory, attract a mate, or warn of danger. It may have evolved to the use of specialized grunts to symbolize important happenings or characteristics of the environment—food, water, a place to hide from the elements, etc. With these specialized symbols available, humans could begin to formulate and communicate increasingly complex thoughts, such as better descriptions of the land across the mountains or how to hunt wild boar. Together with man's evolving ability to use tools, this would have enhanced the biological advantage of intelligence, thus encouraging the evolution of greater intelligence. This in turn would make more complex language possible, continuing the process.

High intelligence is intimately connected with the ability to communicate complex ideas, with descriptions of the surroundings among the more important types of ideas communicated in the early evolutionary stages. In man, the form that this communication took was language, because the mode available for communication (acoustic) was different from the principle mode of perception used (visual imagery). If someone who went over the mountains wanted to tell his group about it, he had to use abstract symbols (words) to describe the water, game, or other things he had seen there.

The dolphin's situation is quite different. Dolphins communicate using the same acoustic sense with which they perceive, and they are probably capable of directly transmitting imagery from one dolphin to another. They have the ability to communicate, in other words, in a manner which would be analogous to direct transmission of visual imagery from one human mind to another. Dolphins construct their images of the environment from the pair of acoustical waveforms arriving at their two acoustic receptors. (Similarly, we can reconstruct the sound of a full symphony, or of a train rumbling past, from the two channels of a stereo recording.) Dolphins also have two separate sound producing organs which they can use together as well as independently. They can thus transmit as well as receive stereophonically.

Think about a dolphin who has been the underwater equivalent of over the mountains and who wishes to tell her peers about the experience. She doesn't need to pick out a few important elements of the experience to represent symbolically; she can share the full experience. By stereophonically reproducing the waveforms she received while she was echo-locating, she can communicate the full acoustic image of what she "saw," placing it directly in the minds of those she is communicating with. She could also selectively filter and interpret that experience, highlighting aspects of it she wishes to emphasize and playing down aspects she wishes to deemphasize, in much the same way that an accomplished cinematographer or animator does with film. With such a capability, there would be no need for the kind of linear symbolic representation we know as language. Why bother with a word (a symbol) for "fish," for example, if whenever I want to tell you about a fish, I can place its image directly in your mind?

We don't know for sure that dolphins do this. Understanding and interpreting their communications lies far beyond current human capability. We do know that they communicate, however, and that they communicate varied and complex patterns of sound. Some of those patterns begin as a tone whose pitch rises linearly with time, then turn into much more complex waveforms. And this is just what we would expect from a dolphin reproducing the pattern of interference between a slash call and its echo.

Humans use language for far more than simple descriptions of our surroundings. We think and communicate about abstract ideas—mathematics, philosophy, politics, etc.—as well as about feelings and emotions. We have no way of knowing whether dolphins think about similar subjects or not. But the medium they have for thought and communication is certainly rich enough to support such thoughts. When we think about how far man has come starting with a series of grunts, the possibilities open to species with larger brains and the ability to manipulate and communicate three-dimensional imagery seem awesome.

In some ways this discussion of cetacean perception and

communication has been a diversion from the main subject of this book, which is human perception. In other ways, however, it is highly relevant. It can be difficult to appreciate the importance of aspects of our experience for which we never see any alternative. Our use of language is like that, a constant and pervasive part of our thought process just flowing along in the background, so to speak. We normally pay little attention to it or to its role in the way we experience the world. By examining alternatives, such as the very different linguistic structure of Hopi and the nonlinguistic mechanisms available to the dolphins and whales, we can increase our awareness of the role that language plays in our awareness of and understanding of the world around us.

3

The Structure of the Mind

Mind is a term that everyone readily understands but that turns out to be extremely difficult to define with precision. The mind is intangible with no clearly delineated structure or boundary. We cannot lay it out on the dissecting table for direct examination, but must infer its nature on the basis of partial and incomplete information. Yet understanding the mind, at least partially, is necessary if we want to understand how we perceive, interact with, and indeed construct, the world we live in. This chapter will briefly examine the nature of the mind and look at some of the mental processes which contribute to it.

A good place to start is with subjects who have had the two halves of their brains surgically split. Appearing superficially normal in ordinary surroundings, these people have in fact had their minds radically altered. In settings which enhance the effects of this alteration, behavior can be observed which at first appears bizarre, until we see enough of it to discern the underlying pattern and begin to understand the lessons it has to teach about the nature of the mind.

Most higher perceptual and cognitive functions are thought to take place in the brain's cerebral cortex. This portion of the brain consists of right and left cerebral hemispheres which are similar in structure but mirror images of each other. Each hemisphere gets sensory input from and controls the motor activities of the opposite side of the body. When you touch something with your right hand, in other words, the nerve impulses from that touch are transmitted to the left side of your brain. That same side then originates any orders back to the hand—to grasp the object perhaps, or to push it away. What you hear with your right ear goes into your left hemisphere, and conversely. With vision, it is not the left and right eyes which are connected to different sides of the brain, but the two halves of the visual field. Thus what appears to the left of center in your visual field is seen by the right cerebral hemisphere, and what appears to the right of center is seen by the left.

Until fairly recently, not too much was known about the functions of the two hemispheres or about the role of the corpus callosum, the connecting structure which joins them. In 1940 a neural physiologist observed that the only proven role of the corpus callosum seemed to be "to aid in the transmission of epileptic seizures from one to the other side of the body." A decade later a prominent psychologist suggested (somewhat facetiously no doubt) that its role "must be mainly mechanical . . . i.e., to keep the hemispheres from sagging."

An epileptic seizure involves the uncontrolled spread of random nerve firings throughout the brain, and the severity of a seizure is related to the number of uncontrolled firings. One treatment sometimes used to reduce the severity of seizures involves severing the corpus callosum, thus preventing the spread of a seizure from one hemisphere to another. The operation produces no noticeable effects on the ordinary outward behavior of the patients, and for this reason was long thought to have no significant side effects. But the operation does significantly affect the patient's internal functioning. Normally, each hemisphere can keep track of what the other is doing or can obtain needed information from the other using the corpus callosum as a communications channel. When the corpus callosum is surgically severed, that channel is cut off. Each hemisphere is isolated from the other and can receive information only through its own input channels.

This absence of internal communication has only minor effects on day-to-day living because information is normally sufficiently redundant so that both hemispheres can get most of it through their external channels. We hear with both ears, making most of what we hear available to both hemispheres. We move our heads around enough so that both halves of the visual field see anything of major visual importance. And even though the right hand, say, is connected only to the left hemisphere, the right hemisphere can keep track of it visually.

If the environment is controlled to eliminate this redundancy, the effects of the loss of communication become clear. If asked to identify a familiar object (such as a pencil) by touch, without looking at it, you can do it easily with either hand. But people whose brains have been surgically split cannot. They can identify objects placed in their right hands but are unable to name objects they handle with their left hands. When you ask a split-brain subject what he is holding in his left hand, he will reply that he has no idea, even though the object is a very familiar one. It's not that he doesn't know what the object is. If you take it away and then show him a collection of things which contains the one he handled, he can easily pick out the correct object—with his left hand.

The explanation for this apparently bizarre behavior lies in the fact that in most people, the production of language takes place in the left hemisphere. When the split-brain subject handles the object with his right hand, the sensation goes into the left hemisphere to be interpreted and then verbalized. When he handles it with his left hand, though, the sensation goes into his right hemisphere. The right hemisphere is unable to direct the production of speech, while the left hemisphere doesn't know what he was holding, so he can't identify the object verbally. (The right hemisphere can apparently understand at least simple language, even though it does not produce language. Shown a list of object names, the subject will usually be able to point to the right name, but he can't tell you about it.)

The same thing happens if you show the subject pictures in the left half of his visual field. When asked about them, he claims not to have seen them. And he is telling the truth, at least in the sense that the part of his mind answering the question does not possess the knowledge. Given the importance that our culture places on words and verbal knowledge, one might conclude (and indeed, some earlier neurologists did) that the left hemisphere is the important one while the right is largely dormant and unused.

But the right hemisphere houses important activities of its own—activities without which we would be unable to function normally. The right hemisphere appears to play a major role in our ability to perceive relationships and see things as integrated wholes rather than as collections of isolated parts. This can be demonstrated by a task which the whole person can perform with ease but which the left hemisphere alone cannot accomplish. We may then infer that the task requires functions performed by the right hemisphere.

One such task involves copying a simple geometric figure, such as the cross shown on the left below. A split-brain subject, trying to copy such a figure with his right hand, might produce something like the figure on the right below. He might have all the pieces, the various edges and corners, but they don't fit together in a coherent whole. The left hemisphere (which is directing the drawing) can see all the trees, but can't put them together into a forest. It sees the individual elements but cannot integrate them into an overall gestalt.

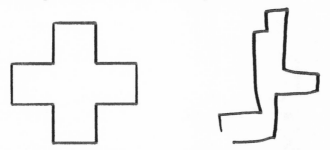

The inability of the left hemisphere to see relationships can also be demonstrated with a block pattern task. Here the experimenter sets up a simple pattern of colored blocks, such as that illustrated below, and asks the subject to reproduce the pattern. (This type of task is often used to screen children for perceptual problems.) The split-brain subject will have great difficulty doing this task with his right hand. He can see which individual blocks he needs but just can't quite see how to put them together. He will struggle with the problem, putting a few together, then knocking them over and trying again.

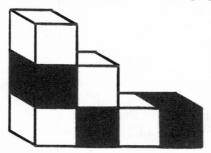

While this is going on, his left hand may become increasingly agitated. It may tap the table, drum its fingers, start toward the right hand and then pull back. It acts as if it wants to help but knows it shouldn't interfere. Eventually unable to resist, it may reach over and do the job. What seems to be happening is that the right hemisphere observes the right hand trying and failing to match the pattern. But the right hemisphere understands the spatial relationships required by the task and knows what needs to be done. Increasingly frustrated by what it sees, it finally reaches the point where it can sit still no longer. It directs the left hand (under its control) to step in and get the job done.

This interplay between the two hemispheres shows up in other ways as well. One of the most striking, in my opinion, involves communication between the two hemispheres using a mechanism which most of us have experienced at one time or another. A split-brain subject was repeatedly shown a red or green light in her left visual field (feeding the right nonverbal hemisphere) and asked to identify it. At first, her answers were essentially random guesses, as likely to be wrong as to be correct. The left hemisphere was answering the question while only the right knew the answer.

After a while, the subject was able to get the right answer most of the time. When the light flashed, she would answer at random. If the answer were correct, that would be the end of it. If the answer were wrong, however, she would grimace and shake her head, then correct her answer. The right hemisphere found a way of sharing its knowledge with the left. Lacking the internal channels of communication normally provided by the corpus callosum, it devised an external substitute. The right hemisphere could observe the light and hear the response given by the left hemisphere. If that response were correct, the right hemisphere was satisfied to let it stand. If the response were incorrect, however, the right hemisphere could initiate a grimace and shake to tell the left hemisphere that it had made a mistake. The left hemisphere noticed this and eventually learned to change its answer in response to the signal.

Most of us have experienced something similar at one time or another—as the "double take," or the involuntary slap on the head accompanied by the sudden realization of something hovering on the fringe of consciousness, such as the "ah-ha" experience. Part of the mind, below consciousness, seems to be using the body movement to catch the attention of another, more conscious part.

THE LEFT/RIGHT BRAIN MODEL OF MIND

What should we make of all this? For centuries, indeed for millennia, men have written about a fundamental bifurcation in the human mind—a separation into two distinct and complementary aspects. Different terms have been used to describe the split—intellectual vs. sensual, linear vs. holistic, logical vs. intuitive, analytic vs. romantic, and even masculine vs. feminine. The terms vary, and different pairs of terms dichotomize the mind in slightly different ways. Nonetheless, the dichotomies seem closely enough related to suggest the possibility that they all describe the same underlying split.

When these various pairings are considered in the light of evidence such as that just discussed, a strong relationship appears. The first adjective in many of the pairs—intellectual, linear, logical, etc.—seems to describe kinds of thought associated with the left hemisphere, while the second adjective in the pair—sensual, holistic, intuitive, etc.—seems to describe kinds of thought associated with the right. It is tempting to conclude that the basic dichotomy underlying all the others is the left/right hemisphere difference. Indeed, a number of contemporary writers have drawn such a conclusion, and the resulting model of the mind as composed of left and right brain activity has gained considerable popularity. We read increasingly of "left and right thinking," about left-hemisphere-oriented people "learning to activate their right hemisphere" and the like.

The left/right hemisphere model of the mind is an appealing one and certainly has some basis in fact. I first became aware of the kinds of evidence I've just presented at a time when I was beginning to think seriously about how the mind worked, and I found that model very attractive. It seemed to explain important and puzzling aspects of the ways people think, and to do so in a way which gave scientific legitimacy to dichotomies which had previously seemed the province of the poet and the philosopher.

As I've thought more about the model, however, I've come to consider it too simplistic, and to believe that when taken too literally it can be highly misleading. In particular, it both relies on and reinforces some common Western assumptions about the mind and about the way things work in general which I now believe are wrong.

The first of these is the assumption that the mind resides entirely in the head—more precisely, perhaps, that the mind is a byproduct of electrical and chemical activity in the brain. The mind uses and inhabits the brain, to be sure, but it simultaneously inhabits other parts of the body as well. Our language contains references to "gut feelings," "knowing with the heart" and the like which we often think of as only metaphorical, but which may have much more basis in actuality than we realize. Don Juan talks of "body knowledge" and tells Castaneda that his body knows things which he (Castaneda) does not. (We will examine body knowledge in more depth later.) Some very successful forms of contemporary therapy, such as Rolfing and primal therapy, appear to depend on the release of memories and feelings stored in the musculature throughout the body rather than in the head. Attempts to explain the mind solely in terms of brain function ignore these very important aspects of mind.

The second questionable assumption is that we can adequately understand anything (in this case, the mind) by breaking it up into subsystems and looking at each of the subsystems individually. According to this assumption, the whole is "nothing but" the sum of its parts. The mind lives in the brain, and what happens in the whole brain is the sum of what happens in the right hemisphere and what happens in the left.

This assumption works well with a mechanical system like an automobile—the carburetor does this, the transmission does that, etc.—but it's not a good way of understanding human beings. As an approach to the study of brain function, it is not far removed from the view (commonly held a few years ago) that particular mental functions and even particular memories were located at specific sites in the brain which could be identified and mapped. To find these sites in animals, neurophysiologists would slice away parts of the brain until a particular function disappeared, then conclude that the piece of brain last removed must have housed the function under investigation. Unfortunately, the sites thus identified were not consistent from animal to animal. The approach is now discredited, and it is generally acknowledged that memories and mental functions are widely and redundantly dispersed throughout the brain and not localized at specific, isolatable sites.

I am not suggesting a total rejection of the left/right brain model, but only a caution against carrying it too far. It has some basis in fact and beyond that has value as a metaphor. But it is not a literally correct explanation of everything the mind does and should not be thought of as such. Ultimately, perhaps, the problem with the left/right brain model is that it is, in terms of the metaphor it provides, too much of a "left brain" model. That is to say, it divides the mind into neat, logical categories and encourages us to believe we understand it in intellectual terms alone, without using the deeper and softer modes of understanding of which we are also capable.

THE MIND AS CONTENT AND PROCESS

I find it convenient to think of the mind in terms of *content* and *process*—the things it contains and the various activities which use, change and manipulate those things—without trying to tie either content or process to specific physical locations or structures.

Under the term *contents of mind,* I would include thought forms such as word-thoughts, images, feelings and emotions; and the mental structures we make of those thought forms— including those previously referred to as perceptual models. The *processes of mind* which manipulate those contents include the various sensory perceptual processes, intellect, intuition, consciousness, the ego, and others we will identify later.

I do not claim that these various categories of content or process have a hard and fast objective existence. They are not like the different sections of code in a computer program. They are convenient conceptual categories applied after the fact to help us to understand a rich and multifaceted part of ourselves which is ultimately far more complex than any model we make of it.

CONTENTS OF THE MIND

I'm going to use the term *thought forms* to refer to the basic elements which fill the mind. The most obvious thought forms, perhaps, are *word-thoughts,* like the ones occurring to you as you read this book. Word-thoughts play a major role in thinking. Indeed, some would argue that words are the basic elements of meaning in our minds—that language is the ultimate repository of human knowledge. These people (including some prominent psychologists) believe that something is not really "known" until it is verbalized in a precise and rigorous manner, and that once that is done, the knowledge is somehow captured by the words forevermore.

I do not believe this to be the case. Most of our important knowledge about the world is not stored as word-thoughts, but as concepts, ideas and related thought forms which are not verbal in nature and cannot be *fully* characterized in verbal form. Much of this nonverbal thought lies below the level of consciousness most of the time, and we have little conscious access to large parts of it. We use word-thoughts to symbolize this deeper knowledge, and are conscious of those word-thoughts as our "thinking." But they are only symbols—tags or markers for the deeper understanding which lies beneath.

Has there ever been an instant when you have completed a thought but did not yet have it fully verbalized? The thing that was completed—before the words were chosen—was a nonverbal thought form. Have you ever gotten stuck in the midst of a sentence—knew what you wanted to say but couldn't find the right word to use? The word you were searching for could not have been the basic unit of meaning on which your thought was based, but only a symbol you needed to express and communicate that meaning.

The mind contains many kinds of nonverbal thought forms, the most obvious perhaps being *visual imagery.* We all use visual imagery in seeing and dreaming, and to varying degrees in our general thought processes. Some people (Albert Einstein was one) do much of their conscious thinking in visual images, translating those images into word-thoughts only when they need to talk about them or write them down. Even those whose conscious thought is primarily verbal may use visual imagery extensively below the level of consciousness.

Each of the other senses also has a form of imagery associated with it—auditory, gustatory, olfactory, tactile and kinesthetic, associated with the senses of hearing, taste, smell, touch and body position respectively. (Kinesthesia, or the sense of body position and movement, is often not thought of in the same category as the other senses. For my purposes here, however, it is similar enough to the other senses to include with them.) We use these forms of imagery primarily in association with the senses themselves and to a lesser extent in remembering sensations produced by the senses—a melody, perhaps, or the smell of a steak cooking.

One can also learn to use this imagery directly, independent of any sensory experience. A musician composing a new melody, for example, may manipulate his internal auditory imagery to "hear" the melody in his head even though it has never been played in the external world. A choreographer may "feel" movement kinesthetically as she creates a new dance routine. The ability to do this with acoustic or kinesthetic imagery is not well developed in most people.

Another category of mental contents encompasses what might be broadly labeled *emotions* or *emotional feelings.* Love, hate, anger, fear, disgust and sexual attraction clearly fall in this category, which might also include feelings of satisfaction or dissatisfaction, of pleasure or displeasure, of power or of helplessness. We generally think of thought forms of this sort as responses to other things rather than as entities in their own right. They do exist independently, however, apart from the things we generally attach them to. There are advanced forms of Buddhist meditation in which the meditator strives to separate emotions from the objects to which his conditioning attaches them, and to learn to see those objects and emotions as separate and distinct. It is possible to feel love or joy which is not connected with anything beyond itself.

In addition, there are thought forms for which we have no specific names. These include concepts of sameness and difference, not always well enough defined to express verbally but meaningful nonetheless. They include holistic under-standings of things as integrated wholes rather than groupings of parts. And they include ideas which we may use words to express but which are nonetheless different from the words and often richer in meaning and content.

As an example of the concept of sameness, consider whatever underlies the word *dog* in your mind. When you see an animal, even one you have never seen before, you can easily categorize it as a "dog" or a "not-dog." You would be hard pressed, however, to verbalize the basis for your choice. And hard as that would be, it would be simple compared with the problem of trying ahead of time, before you see the animal, to verbalize the criteria that will let you distinguish a dog from something else.

This suggests that somewhere in your mind, you have a concept of "dogness" which is not verbal but is independent of any particular words you use to express it. One aspect of this "dogness" is an idea of sameness which sees a similarity between dogs with very different physical characteristics—a Great Dane and a toy poodle, perhaps—but which clearly differentiates dogs from cats. Though you may talk about this concept and use words to describe it, the concept itself is not verbal, and any verbal description of it is incomplete.

These various thought forms are the "stuff" with which the mind is filled. Meaningful patterns and linkages exist among these thought forms. Much of what we know and understand, in fact, is carried by these patterns and relationships rather than by the individual thought forms.

Some of these linkages are hierarchical. That is to say, they relate things according to definite levels of specificity or some similar characteristic. A Great Dane is a dog, a dog is an animal, and an animal is a living thing. Others are simply associative, connecting things in no particular order in ways that depend on how we have experienced them. Great Danes make me think of a childhood friend who owned one and of some of the things we did when the dog was with us. The overall pattern of thought forms in the mind contains meaningful subpatterns, such as all we know about Ethiopia, memories of high school, or our knowledge of how to ride a bicycle.

These subpatterns include what I earlier called our *perceptual models*, the collections of knowledge we use to filter and give meaning to our incoming sensory data and to provide the sensory images we experience as the external world. The pattern of knowledge which allows me to easily identify playing cards flashed before me (and miss a "red spade" in the process), to recognize faces, or to distinguish between different musical groups would be examples of perceptual models.

Though it's difficult to make precise, the mind seems to have a natural dimension of *depth*. Some of what we know seems near the "surface," while some seems "deeper" and harder to reach. This suggests an image of the mind as a pool, filled with thought forms floating at various depths. They don't float around independently, but are linked together in a complex network of patterns and subpatterns. This can be visualized as a set of strings or perhaps elastic bands connecting the various thought forms. Words, in particular, seem nearer the surface, while the nonverbal meanings the words represent are deeper—often harder to see as the distinct entities they really are.

These thought forms do not simply float aimlessly around the pool, but are used, manipulated and modified by a variety of *mental processes*. It is these processes to which we will now turn our attention.

CONSCIOUSNESS

The first mental process I want to examine is *consciousness*— perhaps the most obvious but at the same time one of the most difficult to get hold of. We are conscious beings, and we are conscious of our consciousness. But what does that mean? What is consciousness anyway?

Consciousness, or conscious awareness, can be likened to a light moving across the contents of the mind. We are conscious of those thought forms the light illuminates, unconscious of those it does not. Sometimes the light is narrowly focused—illuminating only a small, sharply defined area, but illuminating it intensely. This occurs when we concentrate fully on a single activity, such as reading a book or responding to some very direct threat to our physical well-being. At other times consciousness may be more diffuse and broadly focused. When you are comfortable and relaxed, for example, you can be aware of your entire body and of whatever images or verbal thoughts are passing through your mind at the time.

In such a state, the line at the edge of awareness is less sharply defined. Like a lantern in the woods, it fades away gradually, its intensity falling off with increasing distance from the center. We can notice things on the fringes of awareness—thoughts not quite put into words. They lurk in the shadows, as if attracted by the light but not wanting to move out into its full glare. Some writers appropriately call this area "fringe consciousness."

The shift between sharp, narrowly focused awareness and more diffuse and broadly focused awareness usually happens automatically, and unless you consciously look it may go un-noticed. The following exercise should give you a chance to see the narrow and broad forms of consciousness and to observe the transitions between them.

Notice your consciousness right now. How much are you aware of at this moment? The book, undoubtedly, and possibly a bit more. But if you're like most people, while you are reading your awareness narrows considerably, focusing on what you are reading and very little else.

The act of noticing itself begins a broadening process. As you notice what you are conscious of, you become conscious of more. *Let that broadening continue. Become aware of more of yourself and your surroundings. Relax. Allow your awareness to broaden further. Feel your body, and let go of any tension. Observe your breath, if possible without changing or controlling it. (That may be difficult, for reasons we'll explore later.) Notice the sounds around you and how the sound pattern changes. Notice that as you become increasingly relaxed, you can be conscious of all these things simultaneously as parts of the whole that is the pattern of your surroundings. You may even find yourself able to "feel" your surrounding environment and your place in it and as a part of it.*

You should now be in a broadened and diffuse state of awareness, and if you were attentive to the process of getting there, you have seen the transition to that state from your ordinary, more narrow focus. The transition back to a narrow focus can be observed with the help of a friend.

Your friend should wait quietly off to the side while you relax and broaden your awareness in the manner just described. When you are in a calm and relaxed state, she should suddenly jump at you, give a loud yell and make a threatening gesture. Even though you know ahead of time that this is coming, your response will probably be an instantaneous narrowing of attention to focus sharply and fully on this new "threat." Your body, your surroundings, the background sounds around you—everything except your friend's body moving toward you and the possible threat it poses—will disappear. By knowing that this "threat" is coming, however, you should be able to save a little awareness to watch the narrowing occur.

The perceptual narrowing you have just experienced is part of the "flight/fight" response, the body's natural and instinctive reaction to danger. The narrowing serves to focus your attention on the potential threat and on your reaction to that threat—on preparation for fight or flight. Potential distractions are excluded from your narrowing field of consciousness. In the natural environment in which the human species evolved, someone responding in this way would have a better chance of surviving, say, an encounter with a tiger. The response was biologically adaptive and probably bred into us by the process of natural selection.

It is worth noting here that a difference exists between *awareness*, which defines the area of the mind you can "see" at any particular time, and *attention*, which defines the place within that area you choose to look. Within the broader field your awareness makes available, your attention focuses on the place of most importance to you at the time. Awareness and attention are related, but they are not the same. The way you use each individually, and both in combination, significantly influences the way you perceive the world. An exercise in vision can help us explore that difference.

Look out at the room around you, without really looking at anything in particular. Notice your awareness of the room and your lack of specific attention. Now focus your attention sharply on some particular thing. Notice how your awareness narrows in the process.

That doesn't really need to happen. You can maintain a broad field of awareness and a sharply focused attention within that field at the same time. Most of us don't bother to do so. Instead, we narrow our awareness in order to focus our attention, so that we don't have the additional effort of focusing attention separately. This is how the flight/fight reaction discussed earlier works. The sudden narrowing of awareness creates a perceptual "tunnel" through which only the threat is visible, thus focusing attention and eliminating outside distractions.

In general, it's more important to pay attention to the direct threat than to any of the distractions, but there are exceptions. If you jump off a high cliff because you've focused all your attention on the tiger, you may not be very far ahead. A better alternative would be to leave your awareness broad and control your attention within that broad awareness, so you could see and deal with the threat without losing sight of the other hazards in the environment.

This can be difficult, especially in a stressful situation, because it goes against strongly ingrained patterns. Such attention requires training and practice, such as might be acquired from the internal martial arts. It is possible to get an idea of what it's like, however, by paying close attention to the way you use your vision.

Pick out some object in the room, and look at it. Let your focus broaden, and see how your awareness of the rest of the room increases. While keeping the same object in the center of your visual field, shift your attention around to various objects in your peripheral vision. Notice that you want to shift your eyes to center the object of your attention in your visual field, but that with effort you can keep the field broad and move your attention around within it without shifting the eyes.

Usually, when we want to attend to something, we put that object in the center of our visual field and narrow our awareness down to concentrate in that area. As with the narrowing which accompanies the flight/fight reaction, this is generally a reasonable thing to do. The way the eye is constructed, our vision is sharper at the center, so we can see what we are looking at better that way.

But there are exceptions. Vision is sharper in the center at the price of requiring more illumination to achieve that sharpness. Under poor lighting conditions, peripheral vision is better than central vision. Have you ever noticed something out of the corner of your eye at night, only to lose sight of it when you tried to look directly at it? Shifting an object to the center of the field in poor light can reduce your ability to see it, or even make it disappear. British commandos learn to sight their weapons out of the corners of their eyes, in order to maximize night effectiveness.

It may seem at times that I denigrate the way we normally perceive things and argue that other ways are somehow better. That's not really the case. I am trying to show that we have different modes of perception available to us, and that the one that works best may vary with the circumstances. We seldom exercise some modes, and as a result we tend to forget them. When that happens we unnecessarily restrict our ability to experience our surroundings. The world becomes a less rich and interesting place than it really should be, and possibly a more dangerous place as well.

Earlier I likened the mind to a pool, with things floating in it at various depths. We are only aware of the thought forms at the surface most of the time—the word-thoughts making up our verbal thought stream, the strong images provided by the senses or intense emotions that may flood into consciousness in response to other stimuli. These "louder" forms tend to capture consciousness, to overpower and blot out the weaker, more subtle forms which float below the surface.

In *The Psychology of Consciousness,* Robert Ornstein draws an analogy with the sun and the stars. During the day, the sun is out and dominates the heavens. Its glare fills the sky and masks the relatively weaker stars. Imagine that you had never been outside at night but had seen only the daytime sky. Imagine that someone came along and told you that the sun was only one source of light, albeit the strongest one, in a sky containing millions of weaker light sources. You might quite reasonably reject that idea.

But the stars are there, and at night when the glare of the sun fades away, they shine brilliantly for all who care to look. If the sky is clear, a telescope with a narrow field of view may screen out enough glare to allow the stronger stars to be seen even during the day. We *can* see the stars when the glare from the sun has faded, and can look into the depths of a pool when the surface is calm. We can also direct consciousness deeper into the mind and become aware of the thought forms which exist below.

Doing this is one of the goals of some forms of meditation. The approach varies with the discipline but usually consists of two basic activities. The first involves gaining better volitional control over the focus of consciousness, allowing the meditator to put it where he chooses rather than passively accepting the dictates of habit and conditioned response. The second involves allowing the high level of mental noise to subside, so that the subtler forms beneath the surface can be more easily seen.

Some people speak of the "conscious mind" and the "unconscious mind" as if they were two separate and distinct entities. They are not. Rather, there is one mind, of which consciousness shows us different aspects at different times. What is in consciousness constantly changes, as the preceding exercises show. There is no "conscious mind" as such, nor any clear line dividing the "conscious" from the "unconscious." There are areas in the mind where consciousness seldom penetrates, barriers we have erected and conditioned ourselves not to look behind. But they result from the way we choose to use the mind and not from the inherent structure of the mind itself.

INTUITION AND INTELLECT

Intuition and *intellect* are two mental processes which are often viewed as somehow opposed to one another, even as mutually antagonistic. I believe this view is incorrect. Intuition and intellect are complementary and mutually reinforcing, and we would be unable to utilize either one very well without the other.

Intuition, as I see it, operates mostly on nonverbal thought forms—arranging and rearranging them, combining them, creating new ones from combinations of old ones and new experiences. It usually operates below the range of consciousness, so we are aware only of the results and not of the process. Intuition is responsible for most of our creative ideas and insights.

The intellect, on the other hand, formalizes our ideas, puts them into concrete verbal terms, and produces and verifies whatever reasoning chains are necessary to support them. It operates primarily with words, numbers, and other relatively concrete thought forms, rather than with the transitory, less well defined forms used by the intuition. It operates much more within the range of consciousness, so we are more aware of the workings of the intellect than of the intuition.

The intellect understands things in an essentially piecemeal way, while the intuition sees more holistic gestalts. The intellect sees the trees while intuition sees the forest as a whole. The intellect is much like our central foveal vision, able to zoom in on something and check out the details. Intuition, on the other hand, is more like peripheral vision. It can't see the details nearly as well, but can get a grasp of the whole which the details alone cannot provide.

In creative problem solving, the workings of the intellect and intuition are complementary. The intellect finds and brings to bear specific facts and problem-solving methods. The intuition searches through our store of previous knowledge and experience for relevant concepts and ideas, then rearranges and restructures those ideas into something pointing toward a solution. The intellect makes the solution concrete and produces a supporting chain of logic and reasoning.

We see the role of the intellect more clearly both because the intellect is a more conscious process and because it produces more tangible results. But the intellect is only the top of the iceberg. Without the intuition operating below the surface, creative problem-solving would be impossible.

Even in areas generally considered highly intellectual, such as abstract mathematics, this interplay between intuition and intellect can be very important. Most nonmathematicians (and far too many mathematicians as well) think of mathematics as the epitome of intellectual endeavor, based on rationality and logic with little room for intuition or intuitive thought. This perception is wrong! The validity of mathematical reasoning is a matter for logical verification or refutation, to be sure. But intuition directs the reasoning and guides the directions which it takes.

In my own mathematical research, I have often experienced the solution to a problem first at an intuitive level—as indistinct imagery of some vague sort, partially but not completely visual. Only after achieving a solution at this intuitive level could I perform the intellectual task of putting together a formal solution and a logical chain of proof. This sort of experience seems to be widespread among mathematicians and among scientists generally. In his book *The Psychology of Invention in the Mathematical Sciences*, French mathematician Jacques Hadamard describes his own understanding of the proof of the theorem that there are an infinite number of primes as a visual pattern of dots of light. He cites other cases in which imagery and intuition have played a significant role in mathematical or other scientific discovery.

In his insightful study of scientific progress, *The Structure of Scientific Revolution*, Thomas Kuhn points out that while the education of a physicist is superficially directed at filling him with the formal knowledge of physics, a major function of the actual process is to build his intuition for the problems that physics addresses. The fledgling physicist spends much of his time performing experiments and solving problems ostensibly serving to drill the formal knowledge into him. But, Kuhn argues, the real role of these problems and experiments is different, and more subtle. They provide the student with a chance to learn what the formal definitions mean in a variety of concrete situations, thus serving as a vehicle through which he can internalize the knowledge intuitively. Without this, Kuhn claims, the formal definitions would remain sterile, and the student would be unable to apply them in new situations.

Among mathematicians, the necessary intuitive gestalt for and about mathematics is sometimes called "mathematical maturity." I became aware of it as something distinct from the formal knowledge of mathematics during my second year of graduate school. I took a course in mathematical game theory for which the prerequisites were calculus and linear algebra, both sophomore courses. The class included graduate students in mathematics and statistics, whose backgrounds exceeded those prerequisites by a wide margin, and undergraduates whose mathematical background was limited to the prerequisites. The former group found the course interesting and stimulating, while many of the latter found it difficult and incomprehensible, and their dropout rate was high.

The prerequisites contained all the necessary formal mathematics, but the students with only the prerequisites had not internalized that knowledge adequately. They "knew" it in a formal, intellectual way, but they did not have the intuitive gestalt necessary to apply it easily. The advantage the advanced students had lay not with their larger store of formal knowledge but with their greater intuitive understanding.

The misconception that mathematics is a purely intellectual activity stems from the fact that the intuitive part lives in the mind of the mathematician and is seldom transferred explicitly to paper. The observer sees only the artifacts of mathematics— the formal statements, proofs, chains of logic and the like—and must infer the nature of the activity from the nature of the artifacts. The conclusion that mathematics is devoid of intuitive content because none is evident in the artifacts is similar to the conclusion reached by the cargo cults that they could obtain cargo if only they could learn to reproduce the correct spells and incantations.

Intuition plays, or should play, an important role in all our thinking. But the Western emphasis on rationality and intellect has caused many people to suppress the intuition, to their own detriment as well as to the detriment of others affected by their decisions. (And when they happen to be government policy and decision makers, that sometimes includes all of us.) This is not to argue that we should rely on intuition alone, unchecked by intellect; but neither (and this is currently the greater problem) should we rely solely on intellect, without the balance of broader, more holistic understanding provided by a well-exercised intuition.

This point was brought home to me several years ago during a discussion concerning a systems analysis project I was involved in. I felt that the approach being taken was overly simplistic and ignored some very important aspects of the problem. One colleague felt I was being excessively critical. He agreed that my objections were valid "in principle," but he argued that the project was being conducted in a way that met generally accepted professional standards, was what the client needed, and was what we were, after all, being paid to provide. He summed up his position by saying, "All you're doing is voicing your gut feelings, Ralph. We all have gut feelings like that, and if we didn't ignore them and go ahead anyway, we'd never get any work done."

That statement clearly exemplifies, I think, what is wrong with the Western intellectual approach to knowing and the technocratic approach to government so much in evidence today. We train too many of our specialists to rely on intellect and formal methodological technique and to ignore (even to distrust) their intuitions. We get specialists who can count all the trees but have no idea what a forest is. As I found myself drifting away from the solely intellectual perspective, I realized that the doubts (the gut feelings) I felt were shared by many of my colleagues, but that most of them distrusted and suppressed those doubts.

THE WORD MACHINE

Just as the name implies, the *word machine* produces verbal thoughts in a steady stream. Other processes, such as the intellect and sometimes the intuition, provide direction to this stream at least part of the time. At times, however, the word machine seems to run on with little direction or control. These are the times at which our thought "wanders," flitting from one subject to another through a series of word associations. We suddenly find ourselves thinking about a totally new subject, because our verbal thought stream drifted in that direction.

The word machine is noisy, in the sense that the word-thoughts it produces fill consciousness and block out the weaker, subtler forms. It is like the sun, blocking out the stars with its glare. For some people the word machine runs almost constantly, keeping them unaware that the subtler forms are there at all. They come to believe they think only in words, because that is all they are able to see in themselves.

Conscious control over the word machine is a prerequisite to the control of consciousness, and hence to any significant degree of mental self-control. Gaining that control is one of the major objectives of most meditative disciplines. This may be done in different ways, depending on the system. In Transcendental Meditation and other forms of mantra meditation, the meditator takes direct control of the word machine by repeating the same word or phrase (the mantra) over and over. This repetitive verbal thought stream demands less than his full attention, and he can learn to broaden his consciousness beyond that stream. The repetitive prayers used by some Christian monastic orders, and by laymen as penance for their sins in some denominations, serve the same function.

In other disciplines the meditator focuses attention on some object of meditation other than the word machine, bringing it back to that object whenever it wavers. The word machine, thus ignored, eventually falls silent except when the meditator chooses to use it. At this point the meditator controls the word machine rather than being controlled by it. Different objects of meditation may be used in this way, including candles, the meditator's breath, mandalas (complex circular found mainly in Tibet), and even body movements such as those used in T'ai Chi or in the meditative dances of the "whirling dervishes."

THE EGO AND BODY KNOWLEDGE

As with the intellect and the intuition, important interrelationships exist between the *ego* and *body knowledge* and for that reason we will look at them together. These interrelationships, however, are not of a complementary nature and are difficult to characterize simply and succinctly.

The *ego*, as described earlier, is the process responsible for the boundary between you and the rest of the world. This aspect of the mind decides what is "you" and what is "not you," and maintains that distinction as you move about in and interact with your environment. It creates and manages your perceptual models of the world, and monitors and controls sensory processes to keep your experience consistent with those models.

The ego caused the failure to see the red spade in the experiment discussed in Chapter 1, because the ego was maintaining a reality that contained no red spades. Your ego caused you to expend energy holding your arm rigid while you thought you were pushing one arm up against the other in the exercise in Chapter 1, thus maintaining your model of the external world as a place where rigid three-dimensional objects act on one another by pushing.

This role of the ego in constructing the appearance of the reality we experience usually gets little attention. We will look at the working of the ego in greater detail later. Another process also plays an important role in our interactions with the world around us—the body's instinctive knowledge of itself and its movements through the world. I will call that process *body knowledge.*

When you reach up without thinking to brush a hair out of your eyes or to scratch behind your ear, your hand moves directly and effortlessly to the place you want it to go. Body knowledge is the process directing that movement. In *Journey to Ixtlan,* Carlos Castaneda describes a way of running which don Juan called the "sorcerer's gait," a kind of "running with abandon," without judgment. Don Juan could run this way across the desert in the dark of night without stumbling or tripping, through areas strewn with bushes, rocks and animal burrows. George Leonard, in *The Ultimate Athlete,* describes learning Aikido (an internal martial art) not by trying to do the techniques properly but by just letting them happen, naturally and without effort. These are examples of body knowledge.

Think about the experience of learning a new skill—tennis, skiing, dancing, golf, or perhaps a martial art. When you first start, your body responds clumsily, and getting it all together at the same time is a major undertaking. But gradually, with practice, coordination improves and things become easier.

Eventually, if you really master the skill involved, it becomes effortless. It takes no *doing* but just seems to *happen* by itself. Your body knowledge at this point has taken over the doing for you.

We generally think of increasing competence as something which comes from a *learning* process in which we do something better and better by doing it more and more often. This certainly goes on, and in the terms used earlier in this book, would correspond to the development of increasingly better perceptual models. But at very high levels of competence—at *master* levels, if you will—something else happens. Rather than learning, an *unlearning* process occurs. You undo the barriers to performance which you as ego initially put in the way and allow your body knowledge to take over.

It seems your body knowledge knew how to do it all the time, but not your ego. The initial clumsiness comes from the ego's attempts to predict and control and to keep experience compatible with the ego's current model of reality (which says, among other things, that you don't know what you're doing). As you practice, the ego's ability to predict and control improves, and so does your performance. You can become technically quite good in this way, under ego control. But you can reach a master level only when you bypass the ego and allow your body knowledge to take over and direct your performance effortlessly.

When the ego does let go and allows the body knowledge to come through, the results can be startling. Tim Gallwey, author of *The Inner Game of Tennis* and other books on sports as meditative disciplines, has a nice trick to put students in touch with their body knowledge. He casually asks a student who is having trouble with her serve, "How would you like to be able to hit it?" Without thinking, the student will react instinctively by saying, "Like this," and serving with far better form than displayed previously. Gallwey may repeat, "How?" several times, with the student responding each time with a demonstration of how she *wishes* she could serve. Finally, Gallwey will pause, reflect, and observe to the student, "Gee, it's too bad you can't hit it like that!"

The ego and body knowledge operate from very different

viewpoints, which accounts for the differences in performance that each produces. Your ego viewpoint sees you as a distinct entity—separate from what is occurring externally. The ego operates by predicting what will happen and controlling your responses accordingly. To your body knowledge, on the other hand, you are an integral part of the world around you, and your interaction with that world is part of the ongoing flow of events. That flow can be allowed to unfold without the need for prediction and control engendered by the viewpoint adopted by the ego.

Think about the problem of returning a tennis ball, as seen from each viewpoint. The ego sees the ball as separate from the player. It must predict the trajectory of the ball, compute the movements necessary to allow the player to return the ball, and attempt to control the player in a manner which will produce those movements. Body knowledge, on the other hand, sees the player and the approaching ball as part of the same ongoing flow. Events can be allowed to unfold, with no more need for prediction and control than would be required in watching a movie, and the player and ball will come together as naturally as a piece of wood floating down a river follows the current.

If you walk across rough terrain with the ego in control, you must continually watch for and avoid rocks, potholes and other obstacles. In the dark, you can't see these obstacles and you stumble. If you can adopt the "sorcerer's gait," however, your body knowledge will guide you smoothly past the obstacles as part of the flow of your movement.

This doesn't seem possible if we accept the conventional Western worldview—which sees the world as made up of distinct objects which only interact according to physical and chemical laws. The deficiency, however, lies not with body knowledge, but with that world-view and with the belief that it really describes how the world works. We will explore the limitations of that view, and look at some other possibilities, in the next chapter.

If most of us attempted to cross the desert on a moonless night, we would find the "sorcerer's gait" impossible to adopt. Similarly, we might find it impossible to play tennis by allowing ourselves to simply experience the flow as the game unfolds.

We might, therefore, be tempted to deny the existence of this kind of knowing and to ridicule the idea that such a way of moving exists. The deficiency there also lies with us and with our excessive ego identification. The body knowledge is there, waiting to be uncovered.

Uncovering that body knowledge is part of the experience toward which Buddhism and other Eastern religions point when they speak of "destruction of the ego," and "discovery of your fundamental nature." The "non-action" which plays such a significant role in Taoist philosophy involves, I believe, a way of interacting with the world through body knowledge, without the ego's attempts at prediction and control. This identification of one's self with the rest of the universe, as part of its ongoing flow, lies at the root of the Eastern idea of eliminating the distinction between subject and object, between the knower and the known.

THE SELF

This brings us to the final process of mind I will examine, perhaps the most elusive of them all, the *self*. Your *self* is you, whatever you are, the process that makes you a distinct, unique individual. But the self has a tendency to continually identify with other processes—sometimes with the ego, or the intellect, or even with one of the various roles we continually play, such as breadwinner, parent, lover or victim. This continual identification with some other process or role makes it hard to see the self as separate and distinct from the things it identifies with, and to understand it in its own right.

But if you really stop to think about it and to examine what "you" are, it should be clear that you are not your ego, your intellect, the various roles you play in life, or even your body. Any of those things could be different without changing the essence that makes you who you are. That you are not your consciousness is harder to see, but on balance, I don't believe you are that either. Consciousness is like the window through which you look, or possibly the light you see with, but it is not the seer.

Buddhist doctrine teaches that there is no underlying, enduring self. I don't understand that doctrine fully, but what it seems to say is that when you peel away all the pieces, the various layers of intellect, intuition and ego, nothing is left. Like peeling an onion—when all the wrappings are gone, there's nothing left inside.

That may be the case. But for now at least, it doesn't seem that way to me. There does seem to be an underlying self which the rest of the processes serve. We can compare that self, perhaps, to someone sitting in the darkened theater watching a movie play itself out on the screen above. The vista will be broad at some times and narrow at others, as the camera angle varies. This corresponds to the broadening and narrowing of consciousness. The watcher may keenly identify with the action on the screen, perhaps with a particular character, and may experience the feelings and emotions of that character as his own. But the watcher is not really part of the action; he is only a spectator, and his identification with the character on the screen is only an illusion.

Observe this the next time you go to a good movie or watch a captivating television drama. Notice how you identify with the action on the screen, perhaps experiencing fright, joy, anger or sexual arousal right along with the characters. Consciously break that identification. Realize that you are simply sitting in a room watching a picture which has no "real" effect on you. Now switch back and forth between these two modes, identifying first with the action on the screen and then with the watcher who has no direct involvement with that action.

So it is with the self, the underlying perceiver within each of us who sees what falls within the light of consciousness, assesses what it sees, and makes choices based on those assessments—albeit with the help (and sometimes the hindrance) of processes like the intuition, the intellect and the ego. Like the watcher in the darkened theater, we may identify with whichever of these processes is dominant at any particular time and think of that process as the self. But it is not, really, and to make that mistake only confuses us and keeps us from understanding our true nature. One of the best reasons for trying to understand these other processes for what they are, in fact, may be that doing so makes it a bit easier to understand ourselves.

4

Perception and Reality

So far I have been talking mostly about perception—about the mechanisms through which we observe and comprehend the external world. I have not said much about the nature of that world per se—about what it's really like "out there." We can examine perception in considerable depth without ever really looking at the nature of external reality, just as we could examine photography or painting without being concerned with the nature of the objects being pictured. Too much initial concern with the nature of objects, in fact, would probably get in the way of understanding the picture-making process. So it is with perception in general.

But now that we've looked at perception, let's shift our focus to the nature of the world we perceive and ask how well that world matches our perceptions of it. Our only contact with the external world comes through our perceptual processes and the images they show us. We are faced with the problem, then, of transcending those processes in order to understand their limits.

To see this difficulty more clearly, think about black and white still photography. Imagine that you have just finished a course on photography and that you understand it thoroughly.

You know how a camera works. You understand how the lens focuses the optical image on the film, how the silver halide crystals are changed by the light, how the exposed crystals are deposited on the film during developing, and everything else there is to know about how a camera takes a picture.

Imagine someone shows you a picture of, say, a tree. There is no way, all your knowledge of photography notwithstanding, that you can tell whether it is really a picture of a tree, or is a picture of a picture of a tree. From the picture alone, you cannot determine this. *The picture of the tree and the picture of the picture of the tree will both look the same.* Very different *things,* in other words, can produce the same perceptual *image,* and that image alone will not tell us which of those things we are seeing.

Now stretch your mind a little further. Imagine someone who has never before seen a real tree or anything remotely resembling a tree. Imagine that his previous experience with pictures has been extremely limited, so that he has not developed the ability to interpret pictures in the automatic, almost unconscious way that you and I do. Think, perhaps, of an Eskimo who has spent his life on a treeless ice floe. Imagine giving that Eskimo some pictures of trees. What kind of understanding of trees would he develop from those pictures? Would he see a solid three-dimensional object or simply a flat two-dimensional pattern of light and dark? Would he comprehend anything like what we "know" a tree to be?

A little reflection should convince you that he can't understand very much about trees on the basis of the pictures alone. He must realize that the tree and the picture might be very different objects, so that to understand one using the other requires a significant interpretative jump. He must draw on several sources of information—verbal descriptions, perhaps, and several pictures of the same tree from different perspectives. He must integrate these various sources into an internal composite understanding which somehow transcends the image he gets from any single source.

If he has several pictures of the same tree, they may look superficially quite different. A picture of the tree from some distance away will not look at all like one taken from underneath looking up through the branches. A picture taken in July when the leaves are full will look quite different from one taken in January when the tree is bare. If he doesn't realize this, he may attempt to find the single "best" or "true" picture and discard the others. This would be a mistake, because only by integrating the information in distinctly different pictures can he ever hope to understand that the tree and the picture of the tree are fundamentally different.

The difficulties we face in understanding the nature of external reality are similar. We experience reality only through our perceptual images; we can't experience it any other way. How can we tell, then, whether reality is essentially the same as our image of it (corresponding to the tree being essentially the same sort of object as the picture); or is fundamentally different, so that we perceive the equivalent of a flat two-dimensional image of something actually much richer? We compound the problem if we experience only a single image of reality (corresponding to having only one picture of the tree), or if we reject other images as unreal because they appear to conflict with our preferred image (corresponding to throwing away all but one picture of the tree).

The contemporary Western world-view asserts the existence of an *objective reality,* a fixed and unvarying underlying structure to the universe which is independent of the observer and, in principle at least, scientifically knowable and describable in unambiguous terms. This world-view acknowledges that individuals and even cultures (particularly earlier "primitive" cultures) may hold erroneous views of reality, but it asserts that such views result from errors in understanding and from a failure to have enough "facts." Those errors are correctable, it asserts, and with enough scientific study we should be able to overcome them and discover the true nature of things.

I believe this view of reality is *wrong!* Asserting that things are essentially as we perceive them (at least if we are careful about our perceptions, as in scientific study) it denies the possibility of important fundamental differences between what really exists "out there" and the kinds of concepts and images we deal with on a conscious level. It confuses the picture with the tree, the map with the terrain. It denies the existence of human perceptual limitations (particularly at the level of verbal description) which are every bit as real as the limitations of black and white still photography as a medium for reproducing living, changing, three-dimensional objects.

An alternative view of reality—which I will outline and which I hope to at least make plausible to you by the time you finish this book—asserts the existence of a "rich reality"—richer, in fact, than the human mind can consciously conceive. This reality continually presents us with many possibilities, a rich menu from which to choose and create our experiences. The experiences we have (and the intellectual structures we construct to explain those experiences) reflect one or a few of those possibilities, brought into sharp clear focus, while the rest remain diffuse and out of focus in the background.

We contact only a small part of reality at any time, but we often confuse that small part with the whole. It's as if we saw only one interpretation of an ambiguous figure like the B/13 or the faces/vase, then steadfastly maintained that it was the only correct interpretation. There is always more out there, always a far richer menu of choice than we can actually experience. Only by realizing that can we escape the tyranny of our perceptual constructions and begin to appreciate the true nature of the world we live in.

This thesis seems to have its own built-in "Catch-22."* It applies to itself, so if it is correct, then the "rich reality" is itself nothing but a model, a partial and incomplete description. Then why bother with it? What point can there be in simply trading one model for another?

Acknowledging a rich reality involves much more than exchanging one model for another. It requires a significant change in your overall way of looking at the world and interacting with it. Belief in an objective reality encourages a restrictive world-view in which one model dominates and conflicting ideas are suppressed. The model is confused with the

---

*Joseph Heller's *Catch-22* was a novel about World War II in which "Catch-22" concerned the criteria for being relieved from combat duty on psychiatric grounds. Anyone who wanted out badly enough to apply was obviously sane, so his request would be disapproved.

reality, and the distinction between the two is lost. The model becomes what Joseph Pearce has called your "Cosmic Egg," enclosing you and cutting you off from the possibilities which lie beyond that egg. If "rich reality" were simply a different, equally constraining cosmic egg, there might be little to gain from the switch. However, acknowledging the possibility of a rich reality can broaden and open your world-view, and help you recognize your perceptual models for what they are and not confuse them with the larger reality they only incompletely represent. This makes it possible to maintain and use more than one view, switching between them and not getting stuck thinking of any one as "real."

This is what don Juan had in mind, I think, in teaching Castaneda about the "sorcerer's reality." This "sorcerer's reality" was another way of seeing the world, quite different from the "ordinary reality" most of us inhabit. In it, the sorcerer could know and do things which were impossible for ordinary people—magical things. And yet, don Juan stressed, these things had little to do with the importance of learning to perceive the "sorcerer's reality." Neither "ordinary reality" nor "sorcerer's reality" was ultimately real; both were illusions. But you could truly understand that, he felt, only when you could see reality in more than one way, and could switch back and forth as you chose.

This is not to suggest that the intellectual acceptance of a rich reality will give you what don Juan was trying to give Castaneda—the ability to switch "ordinary reality" on and off at will. It won't. But it will allow you to understand that such a thing may be possible. Even that is hard to grasp if you believe too firmly in Western objective reality. This, in turn, will allow you to approach the world with a different attitude, to interpret and integrate your experience in different ways. Faced with superficially competing explanations you may feel less compelled to choose between them—rejecting one in order to accept another. Instead you may find it possible to integrate both into a deeper synthesis, seeing each as a different perspective on the same underlying phenomenon.

As an example of what this involves, let's look briefly at something we'll examine in more detail later—illness and the

healing arts. Different cultures have different models of how the
body works and different approaches to the practice of healing.
At first glance these may appear irreconcilable, but when the
problem is viewed in a broader light, they can be seen as
different perspectives on a common underlying process.

Western medicine, on the one hand, sees many illnesses as
being caused by microscopic organisms (germs) and treats those
diseases by killing off the offending microbes. Traditional
Chinese medicine, on the other hand, sees many of the same
diseases as the result of imbalances in the flow of a vital energy
called "ch'i," and applies treatments (such as acupuncture or
moxibustion) intended to rebalance that flow. These different
points of view appear incompatible, and it seems hard to believe
that both could simultaneously be valid. Yet they both seem to
work, providing relief to those who rely on them.

If we view these not as contenders for the complete, literal
truth, but as perspectives on a more complex phenomenon, we
can see that they are not contradictory but complementary.
The body *is* a system of energy flows, and imbalances in those
flows disrupt the body's defenses and allow microbe colonies to
grow. The growth of these colonies further disrupts the flow
and disease results. Both "cures" work! Kill off the microbes
and the body will rebalance itself. Rebalance the ch'i and the
body's strengthened defenses will take care of the microbes. In
either case, the self-perpetuating cycle of the illness has been
broken.

From this broader viewpoint both models are valid. The
question of which was the "real" cause can be seen, like the
question of the chicken and the egg, to be an unreal question
produced by the semantics of language—without meaning in
the world of experience. The apparent incompatibility between
these different models of healing, like the superficial incompatibility between the B and the 13, results from too narrow a
view of the phenomenon in question.

As we soften and relax our need for a single fixed "objective
reality," our attitudes toward other world-views must also
soften. We can no longer dismiss the world models of other
cultures as products of ignorant and superstitious people, living
in the same objective reality we do but not understanding it so

well or so clearly. We must consider the possibility that those cultures bring into focus and experience a reality different from ours, though no less valid. We must also allow for the possibility that they describe it differently, so that their verbal characterizations cannot be interpreted in the same ways we interpret our own.

This does not say, of course, that every explanation of things is as good as every other. All people (including ourselves) are subject to error, and it would be foolish to accept every description of reality as valid. But it is equally foolish to hold that there is but one "true" reality and that perceptions not in accordance with that must be wrong.

Think again about the hypothetical Eskimo and his pictures of the tree. Not every picture he comes across will necessarily depict the same tree. A redwood, for example, is not an oak. If our Eskimo observer were to accept every picture he found as the same tree, he would have a difficult time understanding trees. But of any given tree there are many valid pictures, and some will look quite different from others. If he fails to understand that and throws out all but the "best" picture, his understanding of trees will also be limited. And this is currently the greater risk, given our contemporary infatuation with "objective reality" and "scientific fact" (about which I will have more to say in a later chapter).

By holding too tightly to unambiguous "best" explanations, we restrict our ability to understand the world we inhabit. Some people, for example, refuse to admit the possibility of paranormal phenomena like telepathy, faith healing, firewalking and levitation, in spite of the considerable evidence that these phenomena exist. They do so because they cling to a world model which seems to leave no room for such occurrences. They take that model as reality, and these phenomena become a threat to their beliefs. They reject the evidence for the phenomena, rather than accept the revision of beliefs (learning) which acceptance of that evidence might require.

The difference between the concept of objective reality as it is generally understood and the rich reality I am attempting to articulate here is really a difference in the way we approach the world—the way we conceive of the difference between external reality "out there" and the individual realities we each inhabit. "Objective reality" gives primacy to the external world, granting it an objective structure independent of the individual knower. Things really exist "out there" in this view, and things as you perceive them are approximations of those external structures. Individual perceptions may err, but the errors can be overcome and corrected by careful and disciplined observation. In this way, our collective understanding may approach ever more closely the objective "truth."

The "rich reality" suggests that it's not really like that at all. The appearance that the things we perceive exist "out there" independently of us is an illusion. This does not mean there is nothing there. Rather, it means that whatever does exist "out there" is very different than we perceive it to be. By the time we have processed our perceptions to the point that we become conscious of and able to attach a label to them, we are no longer perceiving the external object at all. Rather, we are perceiving a curious mixture of the object and of our reactions to it, our expectations about it, and our past experience with similar objects. What we perceive, then, is largely our own creation.

External reality may be likened to a rich menu of possibilities. You select from this menu, bringing your personal reality into focus and letting the others fall into the background. As described earlier, you do this largely through learned conditioned responses (like seeing the red spade), unconscious of the process as it occurs. This makes the reality we create very much like that of everyone around us as we are all conditioned similarly. For that reason it appears to be the only one there is—to be "objective reality." But that is an illusion fostered by the cultural consensus of which we all are part.

"Objective reality" and "rich reality" represent two very different approaches to understanding the world. We cannot "prove" one right and the other wrong any more than we could "prove" that one interpretation of the faces/vase figure is more correct than the other. This book, then, will not attempt "proof" so much as it will try to help you bring the world into focus differently—to show you the faces where before you have perhaps seen only the vase.

We will look at familiar things in ways you might not have seen them before, and sometimes at the same thing from different perspectives. Many of the individual pieces of my argument will have alternative interpretations within the context of a conventional objective reality, just as any short section of the outline of the ambiguous figure has an interpretation as part of a vase. What I hope to do, though, is to show these various pieces in a way that allows you to assemble them into an overall pattern in which the rich external reality described above makes sense.

To aid this process I will use some experiential exercises akin to the earlier exercise of getting your arm stuck. As with seeing a red spade, the effects will sometimes be subtle and difficult to catch, and it may be that not all the exercises will work for you. Enough should, though, to give you the general idea. For those which do not, have your friends try them, and perhaps you can find someone for whom they do work and share her experiences.

Some of the exercises you can do alone, and you should try to do those as you come to them. Others require the assistance of one or more friends and may not be convenient to do when you first read them. Don't skip over those, but read them and see if you can imagine the experience. Later, when you have the friends available, go back and actually try it.

Once you've experienced the exercise, or at least understand what it's supposed to do, grant my explanation a hypothetical plausibility. Place it in the mosaic, at least for a while, and suspend critical judgment until the mosaic is more fully assembled. You may eventually find that the most implausible pieces really do fit in, but if they don't you can certainly discard them later.

The attitude of the friends who help you with the exercises is also important—more so in some than in others. If they approach the exercises cynically or as contests in which they win if the exercises don't work, they can make the effects much harder for you to experience—like trying to learn to ride a bicycle while your "teachers" are yelling that it can't be done and you're going to fall over and hurt yourself. The purpose of your friends' participation is to provide a particular type of external stimulus, so that you can experience (and notice) your response to that stimulus. Their intention does matter. In some of the exercises, apparently identical physical motions, done with different intentions, provide quite different stimuli and provoke quite different responses.

5

Experiential Reality

We create models of the world and perceive those models as
the reality they only imperfectly represent. Intellectually, we
build verbal and mathematical models and call them scientific
knowledge. We divide people, nations and other objects into
convenient classes, attach labels to those classes, then think of
the labels as objective characteristics of the objects themselves.
We create perceptual images from a combination of cues from
our sensory systems and from the structure drawn from our
existing perceptual models, then interpret those representations as direct objective images of the external world.

We've considered some of these processes in isolation—
vision by itself, for example, and language. Let's now consider
the way they work together to produce the ongoing flow of
experience which we see as perceiving and interacting with
the world around us. I want to shift from the individual pieces
to the total pattern—from the trees to the forest, if you will.
This will require looking at vision and the other senses, plus
intellect and other processes through which we know the world
as components of this overall flow.

We continually create and constantly maintain an internal

model of the world around us, including our interaction with it. This model, which I will call our *experiential reality*, provides the ongoing flow of experience we interpret as direct contact with the external world. We use this experiential reality to filter and select from the sense data available to us, and to make sense out of what we do select. At the same time, we use the resulting interpretations to modify our experiential reality, updating it to reflect changes as we perceive them.

As I write this, for example, I am sitting in a campground in the Canadian Rockies, and my experiential reality reflects that environment. I am aware of a river flowing nearby, with pine forests on both banks. Beyond the forest on the far side of the river, mountains rise into the sky. I'm writing on a table in the campsite, near the motorhome in which my family and I now live. Other people and vehicles occupy other sites nearby. At least that's the way I experience it, according to my current experiential reality.

To say that I am perceiving a model of the world—not really what's out there—is not to say that the model is "wrong" or should somehow be different. It *is* incomplete. My model represents what it depicts, but it is not the real thing. Only by making this distinction, can we hope to improve our understanding of what external reality is like and of how our perceptual processes constrain and distort our experience of it. We can never hope to learn such things, certainly, if we uncritically accept our perceptions as the reality they only imperfectly represent.

Experiential reality both results from and is the source of my sense perceptions. I know there is a river here because I can see it and hear it. But at the same time, I can see it and hear it because I know it is here. I assemble the appropriate bits of my visual flow into the image of a river and the appropriate bits of my auditory flow into the sound of a river because I know how to see and hear "river" and because a river is a natural and appropriate part of this scene.

It's hard to imagine, right now, how else I might possibly perceive the river. There's nothing else in my experience close enough to "river" to be confused with it, at least nothing I can immediately call to mind. But ambiguities and misperceptions do exist (red spades and B/13). In the forested environment around me now, I've seen a tree stump as an animal at first glance, only to have it suddenly snap into the image of a tree stump as I locked longer.

With hearing, perhaps because we use it less for fine discrimination, there is more ambiguity, and context clearly plays a more important role. Recently I woke up in the middle of the night without immediately realizing where I was. The sound of the river was there—the same sound I had been hearing for two or three days—but I suddenly didn't know what it was. Was it rain? Was it traffic? These possibilities flashed through my mind. Then, I remembered—river! The character of the sound changed. It was familiar now—a river sound, distinctly different from rain or traffic. How could I possibly have confused it with either of them?

We perceive *things,* not sensory patterns. Yet *patterns,* not things, are all our senses can provide. The *patterns* provided by the senses become *things* in our experiential reality. We saw this earlier with the simple patterns of the ambiguous B/13 and the virtual triangle. Look at those figures again. Note that you can easily see the central character as a B or as a 13. But only with difficulty, if at all, can you see it as a pattern of curved and straight lines. See how clear the edges of the white triangle appear, even though there are no objective edges there. The compulsion to experience sensory inputs as something familiar—something meaningful in the context of our current experiential reality—is very strong.

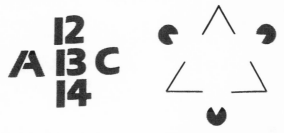

My experiential reality provides a mechanism for stabilizing and integrating the inputs from all my senses and the changes in those inputs over time. I perceive the "river" in front of me, for example, as an object which accounts for my visual imagery of it, the sound that I hear, and even the slight scent of wetness and the coolness of the breeze which blows across it. If I get up and walk around, that same "river" will explain changes in my visual imagery as I move and shift perspective. It will even explain the cold wet feeling on my feet if I walk over and stick them in.

Similarly, the "table" at which I'm writing provides an integrated explanation for the visual experience of seeing it, the tactile sensations which result from touching it, and even the kinesthetic sensation of a solid object which impedes my movement when I come in contact with it.

The individual senses are not the separate processes we usually imagine them to be—each scanning the world in its own distinct way independent of the others. Rather, they are all components of a larger, integrated process, each contributing to and drawing from our larger, ongoing experiential reality. My external senses (sight, hearing, smell, etc.) contribute to my experiential reality, but there are also other inputs. My kinesthetic sense of movement and body position contributes, as does the sense of balance from the vestibular mechanisms in my inner ear. Levels of tension or energy, tiredness, warmth or cold, play a role, as do drives such as hunger, thirst or sexual arousal. The same sun that seems warm and pleasant if my body is cold—if I've just been in the river, say—may appear oppressively hot and unpleasant if I am hot and thirsty.

Beyond all this, however, beyond the external senses and the indicators of internal state, there is more. We each have a direct connection with the world around us, independent of the five senses, which gives us the potential for knowing anything, any time. This connection, which I will refer to as *direct awareness,* generally lies below the level of consciousness. It manifests in different forms and is perceived and labeled in different ways, though the conventional Western world-view would not even admit to its existence. It is referred to as psi, ESP, or perhaps *hunch* or sometimes *vibes.* Don Juan calls it "the lines of the world" connecting everything to everything else, while a T'ai Chi master, using it to sense his adversary's intentions, might describe it as "feeling the opponent's ch'i." It can be seen in Carl Pribram's *hologram,* or in David Bohm's *implicate order.*

Later, we'll attempt a better characterization of this direct awareness, but for now, let's leave the intellectual and move back into the experiential. The following exercise should help you to bring your *direct awareness* to consciousness, and observe a bit of how you use it in creating your experiential reality.

Get your friend who helped you with the earlier exercise. Allow your arm to hang in a loose, relaxed fashion. Notice how your wrist feels. Your friend should now reach out and grasp your wrist, firmly and with strong intention. At the same time, he should say, "That's holding." Then he should release the wrist, saying "That's releasing." Like the grasp, the release should be a sharp clean intentional movement. As he repeats this cycle, observe the feeling in your wrist. Notice the feeling changes as you shift from "held" to "released" and back again. Close your eyes and be aware of the internal feelings, rather than just the sensations on the skin.

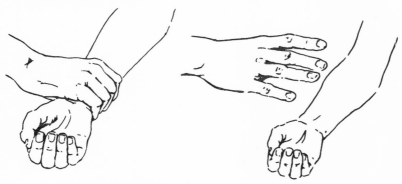

After a few repetitions, you should begin to notice a sensation of *contraction*, a *pulling in* within your wrist as it is grasped. When it is released, you should notice the release of that contraction, a feeling of *letting go* and *relaxation*. That contraction and release were there all the time—from the very first grasp—but it takes a few repetitions to bring them to consciousness.

Once you've found the feelings, tell your friend so and continue to observe them. He should continue with a few more cycles of grasp and release. Then, without any advance notice of change, he should begin to grasp (firmly and with intention) but should stop short of actual physical contact, with his hand perhaps an inch from your wrist. As he stops, he should again say "That's holding," and should project a strong intention to hold. What do you feel in your wrist now?

Most people feel the contraction in the wrist occurring anyway, without any physical contact. He should then drop his hand away from yours, again with strong intention to release, and you will feel the relaxation and release of the contraction in your wrist.

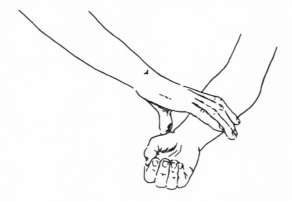

One interpretation of this exercise is that you have learned to tense your wrist in response to the verbal stimulus "That's holding," and to notice that tension. Looking at this exercise in isolation, there's no way to disprove this view. In the larger mosaic I'm trying to fit together for you, however, the exercise shows something much more subtle and profound.

We all have an internal involuntary response to being grabbed! That response, which I will call the *contraction response*, occurs whenever you contact another physical object, and it plays a central role in your interaction with the world around you. Normally below the level of consciousness, it happens automatically without your being aware of it. This response can be brought to consciousness, as we have just done, though noticing it on a regular basis is difficult. The response occurs *in anticipation of contact*, before the contact actually takes place. Your direct awareness of imminent contact triggers it—your friend's intention to grasp your wrist in the exercise. It occurs even when you have no advance warning of the contact through your ordinary senses.

THE ROLE OF THE EGO

You are continually inundated with an immense stream of information about the world around you. This stream includes the information reaching your external senses—the visual flow across your retinas, the auditory patterns at both ears, the full tactile flow across your entire body surface and more. It includes an enormous amount of internal status information—balance signals from the vestibular system, body position and movement information from the proprioceptive system and the like. Beyond all this is your potential for direct awareness of yourself and your environment independent of your usual sensory systems. The total is too large, too redundant, and too disorganized to be meaningful in its raw form. It must be screened, filtered and organized so that you can make sense of it.

The process responsible for this screening and organizing is your ego. My view of the ego has a slightly different focus from the conventional concept but is not basically different. The ego serves, so to speak, as the guardian of the gate, the appointment secretary to your consciousness. It decides what you will see, in what order of precedence, and with what degree of importance attached to it. These decisions also determine what you will not get to see. Your experiential reality is both the result of this screening and the medium through which it takes place.

Your ego also plays a major role in determining how you interact with the reality it has created for you. It acts as your chief of staff, sitting between you (the conscious, aware self) and your body, monitoring and controlling your actions. Like a good chief of staff, this process takes care of details and handles lower order decisions without ever bringing them to conscious attention. When you make a decision and issue a directive for action, the ego translates that directive into the necessary instructions to various parts of the body, monitors the execution of those instructions, and reports the consequences back.

The ego keeps things consistent with its extant experiential reality. If you attempt something not consistent with that reality, the ego will modify your instructions to reflect whatever constraints that extant experiential reality imposes. Simultaneously, it will adjust your sensory feedback to make it consistent with and to call your attention to those constraints. These modifications to your intended actions are so intertwined with your ongoing flow of perception as to be indistinguishable from that flow. This makes it difficult to separate your *perception* of an external object from your *reaction* to that object—to tell which characteristics belong to the object itself and which characteristics are part of your way of dealing with it. And the split we make between those two is often wrong.

To be more concrete, let's reexamine the exercise in Chapter 1 in which you tried to raise one arm while the other arm held it down. Go back and review that exercise. See how you get your arm stuck and seem to be putting energy into trying to move it while really keeping it rigid in space. What happens when you try to move an arm while it's being held in place is something like this. You decide to move and attempt to issue that order. But the ego intervenes, because there's something in the way and the ego "knows" the movement isn't possible. Instead of your order to move, the ego sends an order to make the arm rigid in space and sends a message back to you that the arm is unable to move. You pump energy into the arm and it doesn't go any place, thus "confirming" that the arm can't move because of the external constraint.

Try to experience that process. *Hold your right arm in place with your left, the way you did before. Repeatedly try to move it, so that you feel a little jerk as it tries to move but can't. Doing something over and over again allows you to observe it more closely than you can when you do it only once. Watch the action going on in your arm and bring it into clear, sharp focus. Let's call that action "Action A." When you can see Action A clearly, take away the constraining left hand and continue Action A in your right arm. Your right arm still won't move!*

See that you must do something else to move your arm. Let's call that "Action B." Do Action B, and your arm will move. Without constraining your right arm, alternate between Action A and Action B—between being stuck and moving freely. Repeat that until you can clearly differentiate between Action A and Action B and see that their effects are different.

Hold your right arm with your left hand again. Do Action A. See that the reason you don't move is because you are doing Action A, and Action A doesn't cause movement. Now do Action B. Your right arm should move in spite of the left arm holding it. The left arm will just go along for the ride, because there's nothing else it can do. (If your right arm didn't move, then you did Action A again instead of Action B. Go back to the previous paragraph, and practice differentiating between the two some more. When you can fully differentiate between them and really choose Action B, your arm will move.)

Action B is *moving*, and Action A is *being stuck*. You get whichever one you choose! When you feel stuck, you want to blame it on the external constraint. But the ego is choosing Action A because that action seems more consistent with your current experiential reality. It's that choice which makes you stuck, rather than anything external. Action A won't move you even when there's no constraint, so there's no reason it should move you when there is. To think that it will is part of the illusion that prevents us from seeing our own real power in and responsibility for the world we experience.

The idea of a simple choice between two actions A and B is, of course, a gross oversimplification. *There are no simple elementary actions.* Those we perceive of as such are complex combinations of lower level actions and perceptions. We never simply choose between Action A and Action B. We are always choosing from an infinity of possible actions—involving varying degrees of rigidity, effort, smoothness, and other attributes—and conditioning that choice on the continuous feedback we receive from the world around us.

The important point here is that we are *responsible* for the world we experience, and that a much wider range of *choice* is available to us than we usually realize. The fact that we normally allow the ego to do much of that choosing for us, often in ways not in accordance with our real wishes, does not diminish that responsibility.

SEEING PATTERNS AS OBJECTS

I have already noted our tendency to interpret sensory patterns as external objects, in the earlier discussion of the "virtual triangle." That same tendency shows itself in other ways as well.

In one set of psychological experiments, subjects in a darkened room were shown spots of light moving across the surface of a television screen. When shown two diametrically opposed spots of light moving around a circle, the subjects reported seeing a rotating rod with a light at each end. They mentally constructed a subjective rod as a way of interpreting the lights as the result of an object moving in space.

The experimenters then changed the pattern traced by the lights from a circle to an ellipse. With the lights no longer a constant distance apart, we might expect that the subjects would no longer see them as lights at the end of a rod of fixed length. But they did. They now saw the rod as rotating in a plane tilted by the amount necessary to make the circle produced by the rod appear as the stimulus ellipse. The more narrow the ellipse, the greater the apparent tilt of the rotating rod.

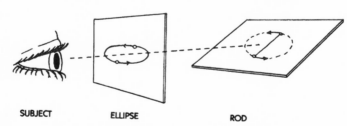

SUBJECT   ELLIPSE   ROD

After reading about this experiment, I had a chance to experience the phenomenon firsthand. I went to a laser light show which included ellipses formed by a rapidly moving spot of light. If I looked at the ellipses in the way I usually look at the world, with my central foveal vision in hard sharp focus, I saw them as tilted rotating disks. If I softened my focus and looked at them with relaxed, more peripheral vision, they became simple patterns of light. Shifting back and forth between hard and soft focus, I was able to shift my perception back and forth from object to pattern. This suggests to me, and other experience confirms, that the tendency to interpret sensation through preexisting perceptual models, rather than to experience the sensation directly, increases as we try harder to "see" and become less willing to simply experience.

Some might argue that this experiment really doesn't show a tendency to construct objects as explanations for perceptual patterns at all, but only a tendency to interpret perceptual patterns in simple familiar terms. We see so many rotating objects, both head-on and at an angle, that the rotating object is the simplest and most familiar interpretation of the circular or elliptical movement. This simplicity and familiarity leads to that interpretation, they would claim, rather than any built-in tendency to perceive a world made up of objects in space.

We do interpret our perceptions in terms that are familiar to us, but I believe the next part of the experiment cited invalidates the argument that "nothing but" that is involved in this case. The experimenters changed the pattern from an ellipse to a rectangle, and subjects still saw a rotating rod. In this case, however, no simple familiar motion of the rod could produce the observed stimulus. The rod must describe a complex and jerky rotation, in which the plane of rotation suddenly shifts each time the tips of the rod arrive at a corner of the rectangle. Subjects quite likely have never previously encountered such a pattern of motion. Nonetheless, the minds of the subjects produced such a motion pattern, and a subjective "rod" moving in that pattern, in order to permit them to "see" a rigid object moving in space.

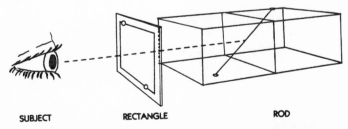

SUBJECT   RECTANGLE   ROD

This same tendency accounts for many common optical illusions. In the familiar illusion shown below, for example, the upper line appears longer than the lower, even though both are the same length. If we think of the lines simply as lines on paper, this seems a misperception, but if we interpret them as representations of lines in space, the perception seems natural. The converging lines give the feeling of perspective, like parallel lines receding into a distant background. Think of them as railroad tracks running off toward the horizon, for example. In that context, the upper line is farther away and fills more of the space between the tracks, and it is reasonable to see it as longer.

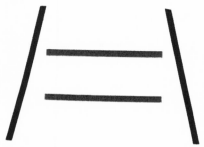

The same thing happens with our tactile and kinesthetic senses. From touching or being touched we get a pattern of tactile contact on the surface of the skin—a slight depression over the area of contact. We translate that sensory pattern into the perception of an external object with mass and solidity. We create this perception by contracting, becoming rigid, and impeding our own ability to move. We then attribute the impediment to the "solidity" of the "object" we are in contact with.

You've seen that process at work in some of the experiential exercises. Let's try another one and see if we can make it a little clearer. This exercise will put you in a situation where you seem physically restrained and unable to move. It will then show you that you are doing things that wouldn't accomplish your purpose even if there were no restraint, then blaming the restraint for your inability to act. This exercise works best with the help of two friends, one to provide restraint and the other to help you remember how to move in spite of it. The one who provides the restraint should be reasonably matched to you in strength.

Sit in the chair (a straight-back chair is best, or a stool) with your feet on the floor. Notice how that feels. Notice the feeling of weight and solidity in your feet and buttocks. Stand up, and notice the shift of weight as you do so. Your weight shifts out of your buttocks and onto your feet, and there is a feeling of "up" in your body as a whole as it rises. Sit down and stand up several times, observing what goes on when you do. Minimize the effort you expend and maximize the feeling of "up" as you rise.

Now, sit down. Your friend should stand behind you with hands on your shoulders to keep you from getting up, holding you firmly and evenly (not maliciously and not trying to make it a contest to see who is stronger). Try to get up. Notice the restraint and your reaction to it. In response to feeling stuck, you push your

buttocks into the chair so you can push back against your friend. You probably pick your feet up slightly off the floor in order to push your buttocks harder into the chair.

Once you have brought your actions into focus, your friend should let go of your shoulders. Don't change what you're doing. Keep your feet up and push your buttocks into the chair as hard as you can. See that as long as you keep doing that, you'll never get up. You're doing something totally ineffective and blaming your friend for the fact that it doesn't work. That's perfectly clear when no one is holding you. Why is it so hard to see while you're being held?

Your friend should now hold you down again, firmly and evenly. Instead of trying to get up, just recall what actually getting up *felt* like. Your weight shifted forward off your buttocks and onto your feet. There was a feeling of "up" in your body as you stood. See if you can recreate that feeling, and then actually stand up without pushing into the chair or into your friend's hands.

You may be able to get up that way, with no more effort than it took when you weren't held. If you can't, it's because the distraction caused by your friend's hands on your shoulders proves too strong. In this case, your second friend should provide a counter distraction. While your first friend holds you down, your second should stand in front of you and extend his hands as if to guide you up. Reach out and touch him lightly, and get up. Don't try to grab his hands or use them to pull yourself up. Just use them as a focal point, a place to put your intention and get your direction from instead of the hands on your shoulders.

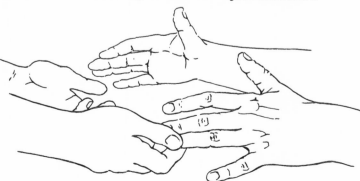

As you shift your attention away from being held and onto the process of getting up, you should rise easily and effortlessly in spite of the hands on your shoulders. You may feel that your friend suddenly stopped holding you down; and she may feel somehow caught off guard, that you got up before she had a chance to react.

Before we leave this exercise, try one more variation. Sit down, and remember how you tried to get up when you felt constrained. Lift your feet off the floor, and push your buttocks into the chair. Notice how foolish that feels as a way of getting up when you're not being held. Continue to do that while your friend puts her hands on your shoulders and pushes down.

When her hands touch your shoulders, notice how the feeling of foolishness evaporates. The same actions that just felt stupid suddenly feel natural and appropriate. But if those actions wouldn't get you up when no one was holding you, they won't get you up when someone is. They are still just as foolish, and the feeling that they're what you must do to get up is an illusion.

The solidity you feel when your friend puts her hands on your shoulders, or for that matter, when you contact any "solid object," is not the fixed and immutable characteristic of external reality that you normally think it to be. Rather, it is a characteristic of the way you connect with reality. It comes about, at least in part, because it is what you expect, what you know how to perceive.

We are so thoroughly conditioned to react to the world in ways that maintain mass and solidity that we have no other mode of interaction. The idea that solidity and resistance to movement are immutable characteristics of the external world is a powerful one and difficult to call to question.

Yet it does seem necessary to call it into question. If solidity and resistance to movement were truly characteristics of the external world, we should experience them always and without exception. Not *most of the time*, but *always*, without exceptions. But there are exceptions. The exercises presented here have shown some. Others occur in the course of everyday experience. Some are spectacular, like the kid who lifted an automobile which had slipped off a jack and pinned his father. Most are relatively minor, like the stuck jar that suddenly opens when your attention momentarily shifts to a noise outside. The ego quickly patches these exceptions over most of the time. You don't even notice they occurred, or if you do, you give them some innocuous consensus-reality explanation. They are there nonetheless, minor "cracks in the cosmic egg," to use Joseph Pearce's metaphor, giving you a chance to see more than consensus reality.

The ability to create these cracks and experience the world in different ways can be cultivated and trained. At the pinnacle, perhaps, are the T'ai Chi masters who can flip an opponent away as if he were weightless, or the accomplished shamans in cultures where real magic is practiced. On a lesser scale, some of the exercises presented earlier have given you the opportunity to consciously open such a crack for yourself.

Learning to increase voluntary control over your experience does not have to be the arduous esoteric accomplishment it is sometimes made out to be. It can be simple, mundane and practical. Several months after reading an earlier draft of this chapter, a woman I know thanked me for the "nice trick in the book for opening jars." She had turned the comment I made about jars coming open when you are distracted into a volitional technique. When a jar wouldn't open she would try hard for a minute, then flick her attention away and open the jar without effort.

PLATO'S CAVE REVISITED

More than two thousand years ago, the Greek philosopher Plato compared our perception of reality with shadows on the wall of a cave. It is, he said, as if we are sitting in a cave, looking at the back wall. Behind us, at the entrance, there is a fire. Between us and the fire, people move about and events are taking place. We see the shadows cast by these events, but cannot turn around to see what casts them. We think the shadows are all there is, and take them for reality.

This metaphor is basically correct, though incomplete. We are not the passive observers it paints but active participants in the process. We ourselves cast shadows and observe our own shadows among the others on the wall. It is the interplay between the other shadows and our own which we have come to think of as our experience. To maintain the illusion that the shadows are reality, we have developed elaborate rules governing their behavior. Shadows of distinct objects must remain distinct, for example. They may touch but must not overlap. If your shadow comes in contact with another, you must stop and hold yourself (and hence your shadow) rigid while a way is found to resolve the conflict. Some earlier exercises illustrated the results of that procedure.

The ego is responsible for monitoring and enforcing these rules, which have themselves become so ingrained in us that we take them for reality. We see them as imposed on us by the world "out there" rather than as rules we choose to follow to give that world the structure we expect it to have. Mistakes do happen and violations of the rules do occur, but we try to look the other way and pretend not to notice. If we're successful, the illusion is maintained and the shadows remain our reality.

The ego controls the information available to consciousness in order to maintain our current experiential reality. We never even notice most of the information available through our senses, and have almost no conscious access to our direct awareness. When anomalies do occur they go unnoticed, or we attribute them to "coincidence" or call them "psychic experiences." Some people (and some cultures) are more open to such experiences than others. Anomalies are more likely to occur during periods of extreme stress (including stress which the individual is not consciously aware of, such as the death of a loved one in a distant place).

We do not perceive the world in emotionally neutral terms. The stored models from which we build our experience contain emotional reactions and value judgments as well as descriptions. When these models are called forth in response to outside stimuli, this baggage comes along with them. A song may stir pleasant memories, the sight of a particular individual might cause anger or fear, or the sight of blood may cause nausea. The ego is, in effect, bringing past judgments to consciousness along with the new information, as an efficient chief of staff should.

The contraction response which we use to create the illusion of solidity is a protective response—intended to ward off a threat, or to isolate and contain damage or intrusion. We use it to contain pain, psychic as well as physical. But sometimes it does its job too well—cutting us off from threats which no longer exist, and from pains which are not as damaging as the cumulative layers of contraction we build up to hide them. These cumulative layers become what Wilhelm Reich has labeled "body armor" and what Arthur Janov's patients are unraveling when they experience their "primal pain."

Much more could be said about these aspects of our experiential reality, but in the interests of balance between this and other related subjects, it seems best to leave these questions and move on.

The ego as I have described it may seem a very different entity than the ego of Freud and conventional psychology. That difference is more apparent than real and comes about because I am focusing on a different aspect of its functioning. By any description, the ego defines and maintains the boundary between the individual and the rest of the world—between the "inside" and the "outside." The conventional view sees the physical aspects of that boundary and the structure of the external world as more or less given. It concentrates, therefore, on the role of the ego in defining and maintaining our internal structure. I see the boundary and the external structure as much more plastic and malleable, and so give more attention to those aspects of the ego's functioning.

After reading an earlier draft of this chapter, my wife remarked that the ego seemed to come across as the "bad guy." It really shouldn't be thought of in that light. The ego performs an important function, albeit basically an administrative one. It handles a large number of details, leaving the self free to attend to other matters. Imagine how much more effort life would be if you had to consciously be aware of everything in your immediate vicinity all the time.

Think of the ego, then, as an administrator, a bureaucrat. Like many bureaucrats, it has a useful function to perform and it performs that function conscientiously. But, like other bureaucrats, the ego sometimes has a hard time putting that function in perspective in a larger context, and it will do whatever it can to see that function given first priority. To this end, the ego will do its best to arrange your life so that it can "do its thing" smoothly and easily. Most of your life you've cooperated, by identifying yourself with the ego and accepting its definition of reality. If you don't like the results, don't blame your ego. It has, as the old saying goes, "just been doing its job."

6

Science
as a Form of Perception

In this culture, we have come to view science as our most authoritative source of knowledge about the world—the standard against which other explanations should be measured. Much of what I've been saying has a distinctly "unscientific" ring to it, making it questionable to some, perhaps, in the light of that authority.

My approach is nonscientific because I am addressing issues which transcend the limits of the mode of inquiry we call science, dealing with and calling into play forms of understanding not usually recognized in scientific discourse. That does not make them non-issues, nor does it diminish their importance. But it does suggest, in view of the authority usually granted to scientific knowledge, that it might be useful to examine the scientific enterprise and place it in a proper perspective.

Science is a form of perception, a way of looking at the world and giving sense and organization to what we see. But it does not provide any unique access to *truth*. The belief that it does stems from an erroneous understanding of what science is about. Science can be, and is, a useful way of obtaining some types of knowledge, and of dealing with some questions. But it has limitations, and will serve us better in the long run if we understand and appreciate those limitations.

What is science, and what is scientific knowledge? The simplest answer to that question, perhaps, is that science is a form of human activity; it is what scientists do. Scientific knowledge is the product of that activity, in the same way that paintings and sculpture are the products of art, and casualties and rubble are the products of war. And who are the scientists? Why, they are the people who do science, of course.

That definition may seem circular, and it is. It is also the least artificial definition I can think of and the one against which others must ultimately be tested. Science can be described in other terms—abstract and idealistic terms, with a precise, scientific sound to them—and often is. Unless those descriptions reflect the way the process of science actually works, however, they describe not science but something else—what their authors think science should be, perhaps, or wish that it were. But they do not describe science as it occurs in practice, and that is what concerns us here.

One such description might be called the *storybook image* of science as a cumulative process of objective inquiry into the nature of things, unimpeded by emotion or human subjectivity, moving always forward, ever closer to ultimate *TRUTH*. Most of us grew up with that image, learning it first as children and having it continually reinforced throughout our formal education and beyond. Those of us educated as scientists, particularly, found that image a pervasive part of our scientific education.

It's a nice image, and it makes one proud to be a scientist. It helps to attract the kind of bright, able people which the scientific community needs, and to indoctrinate those people with ideals and attitudes which have served that community well over the years. It also contributes to the prestige of science and scientists in the public mind, making it easier to obtain continuing public support for scientific research. But the image has little actual or historical basis in fact. It might more properly be called a myth, like the story of Santa Claus. Indeed, it serves functions often served by myths, such as embodying and transmitting group ideals. Taken for fact, which it is not, it produces the misconception that science has some unique handle on truth, and makes "unscientific" a pejorative term.

What, then, is science really like? One of the best answers to that question, I believe, is that given by historian of science Thomas S. Kuhn, author of *The Structure of Scientific Revolution.* Kuhn sees long periods of what he calls "normal science," interrupted from time to time by "scientific revolutions." During periods of normal science, research goes forward in an orderly way—a cumulative process pushing forward the limits of knowledge, building systematically on what has gone before —much as described by the storybook image. Revolutions, when they occur, are periods of instability and disorder. The concepts and rules which guided normal science break down, to be replaced by the new concepts and rules which will again guide normal science after the revolution. The replacement of Ptolemaic with Copernican astronomy was a scientific revolution, as was the replacement of Newtonian with Einsteinian mechanics.

The revolution is not so much a step closer to truth (as it might be described by the storybook image). Rather, it represents a step sideways, to see truth from a different angle. Scientific revolutions involve a shift in world-view, Kuhn says, so that "after a revolution, scientists are responding to a different world." The discipline involved then rewrites its history to obscure that fact, making the earlier world-view appear as an incomplete version of the current view. This continual rewriting of history following periods of upheaval gives science the appearance of an orderly cumulative process, supporting and reinforcing the storybook image.

Normal science is possible, according to Kuhn, because of the existence of unifying *paradigms* which serve to define and guide the research of the various scientific disciplines. These paradigms encompass what we normally think of as scientific theory, but they are more. A paradigm provides a way of looking at the world and how it works—at least that portion of the world of professional interest to members of the discipline the paradigm serves.

Paradigms may arise from particular past scientific

achievements, and from the theory, applications and even instrumentation which flow from those achievements. Newtonian mechanics, Copernican astronomy, wave optics, and the phlogiston theory of combustion would be examples of scientific paradigms.

A paradigm gives the scientists who embrace it a common view of their discipline and the nature of their research. It defines what is known and what is yet to be discovered. It identifies those questions which are fit subjects for research, and distinguishes them from those which are not, for whatever reasons. It even prescribes the types of data which are to be regarded as "facts" and the kinds of observation and instrumentation which may be used to collect those "facts." It provides criteria for the validation of research results, and otherwise guides the research of the discipline.

The paradigm is like an incomplete map, outlining the general characteristics of a region but leaving many of the details yet to be filled in. Normal science fills in those details, extending the map into known but yet uncharted regions in accordance with well-defined rules on matters such as the type of coverage and the features to be shown. In terms of our earlier object/picture analogy, the paradigm can be likened to a point of view—a particular place from which to view the discipline in question. Normal science pictures the discipline from that point of view, with ever-increasing detail and precision.

In the storybook image of science, theories are continually tested against new observations. Whenever facts are uncovered which disprove the theory, it is thrown out. This doesn't really happen, according to Kuhn. Theories (and their accompanying paradigms) are never discarded simply because they don't agree with the facts, unless the disagreement has become too blatant to ignore and a satisfactory alternative explanation has become available.

There are always questions which a scientific theory can't answer, data which can't be interpreted in the context of the current paradigm, observations which simply "don't fit." For a while, these anomalies can be ignored, and normal science proceeds as though they didn't exist. Attention focuses on questions which the paradigm can deal with, and on broadening and extending knowledge as the paradigm defines it. With time, the anomalies become harder to ignore, creating increasing problems for the conduct of normal research. Crisis develops, leading to the period of transition which Kuhn calls *scientific revolution*. A whole field of science may be affected or just a small subdiscipline. Similar mechanisms operate in either case.

The methods and procedures which have guided normal science in the affected discipline begin to break down. Workers in the field devote more attention to the anomalies and to their resolution. The more innovative researchers find old ways of looking at things inadequate and begin to search (consciously or unconsciously) for new perspectives which will resolve the difficulties. New ways of seeing the problems are found, and some develop into schools of thought strong enough to compete with the existing paradigm. Eventually one may emerge as the new, dominant paradigm, replacing the one found wanting. Another period of normal science follows, now guided by that new paradigm. Research again becomes an orderly, cumulative process, extending the detail in the map that paradigm provides. The beginnings of this process can be seen today in the "new physics" of physicists such as Fritjof Capra and David Bohm, though the challenge is not yet strong enough to be clearly called a revolution.

During periods of normal science, consensual rules and procedures exist to guide research, resolve disputes, and otherwise keep the process tidy. During scientific revolutions, these rules and procedures do not operate. Indeed, the points of difference between competing paradigms often involve questions about those rules—about what constitutes fact, for example, or what research methods and procedures are legitimate. The "new physics" calls some very basic assumptions into question, including the separation between the observer and the phenomenon under observation and the premise that the material world can be explained without reference to consciousness. If this challenge to existing orthodoxy succeeds, it will bring about a fundamental change in the nature of scientific practice. In scientific revolutions, as in political ones, ordinary organs of authority break down and the revolution must be resolved by extraordinary means. The ultimate victory of the new paradigm may depend on a number of factors, including aesthetics and even the personal prestige of proponents on various sides, but it will not come solely from logic and cold hard fact.

Neither of the competing paradigms, in all probability, will show clear superiority in any objective sense. The new one will look better to its proponents because it resolves the anomalies which precipitated the crisis; but it will have clear flaws of its own, questions it cannot answer that the old paradigm dealt with easily. It may have many of these, in fact, since it is new and not yet very fully developed.

During the eighteenth century, for example, chemists believed that flammable materials contained a substance called *phlogiston*, which was released during combustion. This theory was eventually abandoned in favor of the view that there was something in the air which combined with burning materials. This transition is often described as the "discovery" of oxygen, as though it took place as a single event. It did not. It took place gradually as laboratory experimentation and changes in other areas of science resulted in a growing body of evidence which could be explained within the phlogiston theory only with increasing difficulty. One of the first chemists to isolate oxygen in the laboratory, Joseph Priestly, never did accept the fact that he had found a distinct substance. Rather, he believed that he had isolated "dephlogistonated air," air with the phlogiston removed. His perceptual models could not show him the substance we now understand as oxygen, so he did not see it.

One issue with which the phlogiston theory was better able to deal than was the oxygen theory concerned the common properties of metals, and the question of why various metals share more common properties than the ores they come from. From a phlogiston perspective, the metals themselves result when the ores are combined with phlogiston, so the common properties are derived from that phlogiston. When the ores are viewed as metallic oxides, that explanation doesn't work. Indeed, one would expect the ores, and not the metals, to be more alike. As the existence of oxygen was accepted, this issue, as often happens, became a nonquestion, not fit for a scientist to concern himself with. Not until much later, with the development of the periodic table of elements, did it again become a legitimate scientific question.

Once the revolution is over, Kuhn claims, the world is changed, at least for the scientists involved. Where before combustion released phlogiston, it now consumes oxygen. Where before the sun revolved around the earth, the earth now revolves around the sun. Kuhn compares it to a gestalt shift of perspective, to "seeing a rabbit where there once was a duck," referring to a visual illusion similar to the faces/vase illusion we looked at earlier. The revolution may affect the discipline as a whole more radically than its individual members, Kuhn points out. Older scientists may find themselves unable to make the switch (as was Priestly). But younger scientists entering the field gradually adopt the new paradigm, while adherents of the old eventually die out.

After the revolution, the process of rewriting history begins. It happens as part of the process of scientific education, without conscious intent to deceive. New scientists are taught to see the world as their discipline sees it, to participate in the ongoing process of normal science. Scientists develop their knowledge of the history of science from studying science, not history, and the general public gets its knowledge of science from the scientists.

Textbooks are written to help the student see the world as the discipline now sees it, from the perspective now considered "correct." History is treated from a contemporary rather than a historical perspective. What came before is presented in the context of its contribution to contemporary science, not in the context of its own time and place. Isaac Newton's interests in alchemy and mysticism are seldom mentioned, for example, for those are not now subjects of concern to a "proper scientist." The past is shown as prologue to the present, and science as a whole appears as an orderly, cumulative process.

In terms of our object/picture analogy, think of the world "out there" as a cluttered and complex scene. Normal science is comparable to the process of making a detailed drawing of the scene from one particular point of view. Many artists work on the picture, each filling in here, adding details there. Certain elements of the scene may be difficult to see from the chosen viewpoint. Something else may obscure them, or it may be just a bad angle for them. While the work concentrates on details which are clearly visible, this causes no real problem. But as those details are filled in, difficulties in representing the hard-to-see parts of the scene become more pressing.

Eventually, some artists begin to realize that they could work better from a slightly different position. The rules that require working from only the existing viewpoint begin to break down. A few artists find that the whole scene looks better from a different perspective. They shift to that new perspective and try to recruit others to join them. Older artists with a great deal of investment in the old viewpoint are unlikely to make the switch; but if enough new ones can be recruited, the perspective of the overall picture will shift.

As the picture begins to take on the new perspective, some of the work already done will need modification. Certain elements of the picture will look almost the same from both perspectives, requiring only a minor touchup. Other elements which were visible from the old perspective may now be obscured. These must be painted over and removed from the scene. Elements visible from the new perspective but not from the old will have to be added.

New artists who come to work on the picture will be trained to see the scene from the new perspective only. They will be taught to appreciate the work of past great artists, but only as contributors to the picture which now exists. The work of those past artists, therefore, will be presented to them as imperfect attempts to represent the scene from the current viewpoint, rather than from a different, now discarded perspective. They will come to see the entire history of the picture as a continuing cumulative effort to depict the scene "objectively," which is to say, from the current viewpoint, in ever greater detail.

My first exposure to the idea that scientific training might be limiting rather than broadening came during a long evening of beer drinking and philosophizing when I was a graduate student. A friend who was studying physics suggested that perhaps we were not really learning to see the world openly and objectively, as we were being taught to believe, but to see it in a particular way and to be blind to things which didn't accord with that way of seeing. I was far from ready to accept such a radical idea and said I really didn't think that was the case. He didn't think so either, but he found the possibility an intriguing one.

I remembered the conversation more than a decade later, when he visited the city where I lived and we spent an evening together. I attempted to show him the new world that was beginning to open up to me and to share it with him. He was interested but skeptical, because so much of what I said conflicted with things he "knew" as a physicist.

The best way to think about science, I believe, is as a perceptual process with a structure similar to that of the other perceptual processes discussed earlier. Like those processes, it involves a matching of models with perceptual cues drawn from the environment, to produce images of selected portions of that environment. The cues and the models are quite different from those present in, say, vision, but the underlying structure of the process is similar.

In vision the cues include the lines, corners, angles and hues from which we assemble our visual images. In science they are fact, data and measurements. In vision we obtain these cues unconsciously as part of our ongoing visual flow. In science we obtain them through conscious observation and measurement, often aided by various kinds of instrumentation.

The models are different, too, as is the process of matching cues to models. In vision the models are internal representations of things we know how to see—houses, trees, the letter B—and the matching process goes on automatically and unconsciously. In science the models are logically consistent verbal and mathematical structures, and the matching process is more conscious and explicit. That's true, at least, of the part of the matching process in which theory is compared to and tested against the facts. There is another side of the matching process which receives far less explicit notice—the unconscious use of existing theory to determine what qualifies as fact and how it should be observed and measured. But in science as in vision, neither models nor cues fully determine one another. Rather, each influences the other in a complex mutual interdependence difficult to represent in terms of one-way cause and effect.

The products of vision and science appear superficially quite different. From vision we get ongoing visual images of the world around us; science provides us with scientific knowledge which can be used to explain, predict and control the world. Yet both are images of reality. They provide order to the world, or at least to parts of it, and a way of knowing about our surroundings in a form we find useful in dealing with those surroundings.

Science has particular characteristics which determine its unique capabilities and limitations. We have already discussed some of these characteristics individually. I now want to review them collectively, and look briefly at the kind of limitations they impose on science as a way of understanding the world—as distinct from predicting and controlling it. This will primarily involve normal science as practiced between scientific revolutions, which is most of the time.

One of the major distinguishing features of science, already discussed at length, is that at any given time it sees a particular phenomenon or group of phenomena from a single consensual perspective, a paradigm. The viewpoint of this perspective is always separate and apart from the phenomena under study. The scientist sees himself, in other words, as a detached objective observer. He watches, records, and studies what goes on, but does not think of himself as part of the process. He views the phenomenon he studies as something apart from himself, something which would happen in exactly the same way if he were not present.

The scientist sees the phenomenon he studies in terms of observations and measurements which have well-defined meanings within the context of the paradigm he works in. He concerns himself with things which are repeatable, in the sense that different scientists using the same methods and procedures will arrive at the same result. Data obtained in this way are considered to be "facts," the perceptual elements with which science operates.

Science takes a reductionist approach to explaining the world. It attempts, in other words, to break the world up into isolatable phenomena—such as gravity, chemical reactions, the replication of DNA molecules—which can be isolated and studied individually. More complex phenomena are seen as "nothing more" than the product of many of these simple interactions. Extreme proponents of this view once believed (and some may yet) that the entire future course of the world could be determined (at least in principle) from the position and velocity of all the particles making up the world at any fixed instant of time.

This reductionist tendency manifests itself in the way that science is divided into disciplines, specialties and sub-specialties within specialties. Scientists become successful, it seems, by learning more and more about less and less. It further manifests itself in the kinds of explanatory models used by science, in which complex processes are explained as the product of large numbers of simple processes. Science seeks parsimonious explanations, based on the fewest explanatory variables and the minimum of interconnecting structure. It is guided by the principle of *Occam's razor*—when confronted with more than one explanation, choose the simplest. Slice away superfluous and extraneous structure; make things as simple as possible.

Finally, scientific explanations and explanatory models are symbolic models—structures made of words and other symbols. The essence of scientific knowledge lies in the symbols which express it, with no appeal made to deeper, non-verbal levels of meaning. The symbolic models of the scientist are meant to be taken literally, to be treated as equivalent to the objects they represent. For this reason different people should (in principle) have no difficulties in agreeing on the meaning of scientific knowledge, assuming, of course, that they understand the meaning of the words and other symbols used to express that knowledge.

Science appears to have been quite successful in providing explanatory models for natural phenomena useful for prediction and control, at least in inanimate areas such as physics and chemistry. It has been successful in areas relating to human behavior. Disciplines such as psychology and sociology, for example, are hardly "sciences" in the same sense as physics and chemistry. Kuhn describes them as being in the "pre-paradigm" stage, not yet having settled on the single consensual paradigm necessary for the conduct of "normal science."

But even in disciplines like physics and chemistry, the appearance of success may be somewhat illusory. We see those disciplines as successful because we take them on their own terms. We judge their abilities to explain and predict the world from the perspective of their own current paradigm. We forget about the succession of past paradigms long discarded, and future paradigms yet to arise (as they inevitably will). We see the questions which current science can answer but are blind to questions which are not visible from the current perspective. Examples of what can be lost in this way will be touched on later in the discussion of health and healing.

What about the ability of science to show us the true nature of things—to help us understand the world as it really is, rather than to predict and control selected phenomena? Is science a good mechanism for that purpose, the best yet discovered, as some of its advocates claim? Or is it of limited value, potentially deceiving if not handled carefully?

The answer to that question depends on the kind of external reality that's "out there" and the ability of a single consensual perspective to accurately portray that reality. If there were a fixed and unambiguous "objective reality" existing independently of our observation of it, then science would provide an excellent tool to describe and understand that reality. This kind of reality is assumed by the storybook image of science, and on the basis of that assumption, the storybook image makes sense.

I have argued, on the other hand, that it's not like that at all. We live in a rich reality. Many possibilities are always present and we each play a major role (albeit unconsciously) in determining how reality actualizes itself for us. The "detached observer" does not exist; to adopt that role is a fantasy. Any single perspective is self-limiting, no matter how strong the consensus favoring it. To consider only observations which are repeatable in terms defined by such a perspective insures blindness to phenomena of broader scope.

Think for a bit about the nature of science as it might be practiced by beings who were totally insensitive to temperature, but who otherwise perceived things just as we do. Consider phenomena in which temperature plays an important role, such as thermal expansion and contraction or the speed of chemical reactions. Where we see order and regularity, they would see disorder and disarray. Objects would change length slightly for no apparent reason, and the duration and intensity of chemical reactions would vary. The surfaces of lakes and other bodies of water would sometimes turn solid, and precipitation would occasionally fall as snow instead of rain. These phenomena might appear related to the length of the day, occurring more often on shorter days. If the beings demanded consistency and repeatability in their observations, such phenomena might remain forever outside the scope of their scientific inquiry.

Sounds absurd, doesn't it? Not at all the kind of order and regularity we have come to associate with science. It sounds almost as bad as the disorder and lack of repeatability some scientists complain of in parapsychology. Could there be a parallel? Could there be factors which play as important a role in psychic phenomena as temperature does in chemical reactions, but to which skeptical scientists are totally insensitive? Psychics sometimes complain that they can't function well in the presence of "bad vibes," of a critical audience expecting to see them fail. Hard-nosed skeptics tend to laugh at such claims, of course.

Factors like the climate of feeling and support from those nearby (sometimes called "vibes" by those sensitive enough to perceive them), or even the need which the person has for the phenomenon, do seem to play a role in paranormal phenomena. The importance of *need*, for example, can be seen in the fact that such phenomena are often associated with times of stress (like the death of a loved one). In the book *Rolling Thunder*, about his relationship with a Shoshone medicine man, Doug Boyd describes Rolling Thunder's ability to find medicinal plants and herbs during seasons when those plants do not normally bloom and to perform other unusual acts "when there is a need." He would be unable to perform the same feats, Boyd suggests, as a "demonstration" if no other purpose were being served.

Science operates in a physical, material context, where factors like mass, temperature, humidity and electrical charge are meaningful, but need, intention, and attitude are not. Phenomena which depend on these latter factors, therefore, appear erratic and unstable. To take those factors seriously would call into question the ideal of the scientist as the detached, objective observer, watching but not affecting the phenomenon he studies. Such phenomena, therefore, are poor subjects for scientific study. But that does not mean that they do not exist.

The reductionist approach taken by science, combined with the desideratum of parsimony, insures that our scientific understanding of the world will be piecemeal and fragmented. The world is parceled out into increasingly finely divided specialties and subspecialties, while broad themes cutting across disciplinary lines go unnoticed. Study the little pieces, the storybook image says, and the larger picture will take care of itself. It is a little like trying to understand and appreciate art by studying paintings with a magnifier a square inch at a time.

Ecologist Barry Commoner has observed that "everything is connected to everything else," though the interconnections may be tenuous and roundabout. The application of Occam's razor, with its admonition to simplify as much as possible, insures that explanations will be incomplete and interconnections will be missed. Splitting things up into pieces and looking for the simplest way of explaining each piece in isolation has proven to be a very fruitful means of predicting and controlling portions of the world, but it is not a very good way to understand things as a whole.

The insistence on precise symbolic (verbal and mathematical) codification of knowledge also diminishes the utility of science as a vehicle for in-depth understanding, in spite of the value of that codification for reasons such as repeatability. Words and other symbols are not our basic units of meaning, but only superficial tags attached to deeper understanding. To symbolize, verbally or otherwise, is to simplify and sometimes to trivialize. By insisting on unambiguous, consensual, verbal codification of knowledge, science limits our ability to utilize deeper levels of understanding where such codification is impossible.

Let me reiterate that this is not an attack on science per se, but only on our failure to recognize and pay sufficient attention to the limits of science and scientific knowledge. Science can be a useful and fruitful way of studying the world and of accumulating knowledge about some of the processes which make it work. But science is not, by itself, a good way to understand the world as a whole. Historian and critic of science Theodore Roszak has compared science to the making of maps. Maps are useful things, he notes, but anyone who fails to distinguish between the map and the terrain it represents is insane.

7

Different Drummers, Different Tunes

The way we perceive the world—the perceptual elements we pull from the background and assemble into the things we see "out there"—depends on the culture into which we were born. Different cultures have looked at the world in different ways and as a result have seen very different worlds.

The currently dominant Western world-view sees the world in largely physical terms. Nonmaterial phenomena like mind and emotion are viewed as the byproducts of material activity, if they are acknowledged at all. No underlying purpose is acknowledged; life is just something which arose by chance from random combinations of molecules. Some other cultures, to the contrary, have viewed nonmaterial phenomena as primary and seen the material world as the largely illusory background against which nonmaterial phenomena occur. They see the purpose of life as being in harmony with the flow of the universe and growing in understanding of the nature of things.

An examination of aspects of the Western world-view reveals that it both reflects and perpetuates its particular narrowness, in contrast with alternatives which have characterized other, sometimes more perceptive cultures. Not that the Western world-view is totally one way and that of other cultures totally another. Life is more complex than that, and cultural world-views are complex and ever-changing mixtures. Still, if we isolate and identify main themes and view them against a contrasting backdrop, we can highlight characteristics of our culture which usually lie unnoticed in the background.

Cultures are usually ethnocentric, believing themselves to be the best yet to exist, sitting at the pinnacle of human evolution. Such beliefs serve to protect the culture from outside influences by encouraging its members to think disparagingly of other cultural alternatives. The Chinese view that people in the rest of the world were "barbarians" and the early Japanese hostility to European explorers are well-known examples. Our own culture is highly ethnocentric. We seem to know more, in scientific terms, than any society ever has. This knowledge has brought us unprecedented abilities to control and exploit the natural world, and previously unheard of material benefits. If we need further evidence of our superiority, we find it in the degree to which others are following our lead, trying to "Westernize" and catch up with us.

We characterize cultures very different from our own, particularly those with low levels of technology and few material goods, as "primitive." We denigrate their beliefs as ignorance and superstition, believing our "superiority" to be the result of a natural upward cultural evolution in which the losers (the primitive cultures) are selected out while the best and fittest remain. The evolutionary analogy can be a valuable one, I think, but we need to develop it more fully. Evolutionary fitness involves an ability to persist, to survive over time. Organisms which exploit their environment too well may appear successful in the short run, but rapidly die out when that exploited environment can no longer sustain them.

Perhaps it would be useful to put ourselves in proper evolutionary perspective. The earth itself is four to five billion years old. Life has existed for perhaps half that time. The dinosaurs, which we think of as evolutionary failures, persisted for over 100 million years. The earliest human remains are perhaps three million years old, while the stream of recorded history culminating in contemporary Western society spans approximately 6000 years. Modern science, the form of cultural perception upon which contemporary society is based, has come into being quite recently, within the last few hundred years. Society as we now know it cannot long endure, because we are rapidly depleting the resource base required for our way of life. It could well end up, as Theodore Roszak has suggested, that in the long run "urban-industrial society will turn out to have been an experiment that failed."

On the other hand, some of the cultures we label as "primitive" have existed as stable societies for thousands of years. They coexisted with their environments on a steady-state basis, at least until the growth of Western society disrupted that coexistence. They did not emphasize the same things we do, nor did they develop in the same ways. But to think that they functioned so well for so long with invalid belief systems, while we, in our relatively short and unstable tenure, have somehow cornered the market on truth, strikes me as the ultimate in cultural conceit.

We base our belief in our own superiority partly on health and economics. Life in earlier societies was, we think, "nasty, brutish and short"—unending toil to eke out a living, culminating in an early death. We find that view confirmed when we look at the contemporary remnants of those societies, and we convince ourselves that only modern science and technology protect us from a similar fate.

The conditions in which remnants of earlier societies live today are bad. The poverty evident on Indian reservations in the U.S., the squalor and disease of an Asian city slum, and the economic and political chaos in some of the newly independent African states provide clear evidence of that. But those conditions reflect the contemporary status of earlier cultures as they now exist in an increasingly industrialized and overpopulated world. These remnants do not represent traditional life styles, but the modern destruction of those life styles following the loss of the "range" they needed, the natural environment required to make them work.

The native Indian population of the United States is much the same today as in, say, the sixteenth century. At that time, however, that population was spread across a continent rich in game, fish and the other resources necessary to support it. Today that same population exists on the leavings of the dominant society, on land the white settlers didn't want.

In their natural environment, these societies fared much better. Providing for basic needs was not an all-consuming task; the average hunter-gatherer probably had more leisure time than you do, not less. (If you really think that people today work a 40 hour week, then remember to add in the time spent commuting, mowing the lawn, washing the dishes and otherwise handling the basic "overhead" of living.) The labor-intensive art and decoration so common in many earlier cultures could not be produced by a society in which everyone worked from dawn to dusk to eke out a subsistence living. Earlier societies also maintained rich bodies of literature, poetry and history. These were often largely oral rather than written, and so were largely invisible to us.

I am not attempting to argue that these earlier societies were utopias. They probably weren't any closer to that than is our own. But neither did they consist of the unending toil and misery we often picture to show ourselves how far we have "progressed" and how much better off we are. These societies saw the world differently than we do, and used it differently as well. They knew things we have forgotten or never knew at all. There is much we can learn from them, enriching our lives in the process. But we can't do so if we think of them as "primitive" and of ourselves as superior across the board. For this reason, I will avoid the term "primitive," with its connotation of "less advanced" and will speak instead of "traditional" cultures, emphasizing their greater tenure and continuity.

One of the major characteristics of contemporary society is its fragmentation. I have already discussed the reductionism and resulting fragmentation in science; similar fragmentation exists throughout the society as a whole. We see areas of our cultural life such as law, politics, science, agriculture or medicine as separate and distinct, with little overlap or interrelationship. Each breaks up into still smaller fragments. The best use for a general practitioner, a physician once told me, is to refer you to the right specialist when you get sick. Our lives fragment along other dimensions as well. It is common for personal life to be completely divorced from business or professional life, with a different set of values and ethics applied (and expected) in each. Religion, if it plays a role at all, may be in a totally separate box, cut off from everything else altogether.

Traditional societies seem to view life more as a whole, and less as a collection of separate pieces. Politics, religion, crafts, and agriculture are aspects of that whole, rather than separate compartments. The kinds of distinctions we make between religion and science do not exist. The same basic understanding governs views of illness and healing and of ethics and of the proper nature of society. Lines between various aspects of life may exist in a functional sense, but they are not the sharply drawn distinctions we find in Western society.

The shaman or medicine man, for example, may combine the functions we attribute to priest, physician, counselor, political advisor and scientist. For a young Eskimo, killing his first seal is an important social and religious event, as well as an economic one. The *Tao Te Ching*, a Chinese classic, is at the same time a treatise on government and political philosophy, an essay on personal ethics and behavior, and a work of mysticism and esoteric knowledge.

Some would argue that the more unified world-views of these traditional societies reflect a simpler culture, in which there is less to know and so less need for specialization. There may be some truth to that, but which is cause and which effect? Does our specialized compartmentalized knowledge produce a fragmented world-view or does it result from such a world-view? Each probably contributes to the other. Here we see that problem of neatly separating cause and effect again.

For that matter, do we really live in a much more complex world than traditional peoples do, or are we simply aware of the complexities we face and blind to the qualitatively different kinds of complexities facing someone who lives in a natural, nontechnological environment? Is it really harder to find a street address on the other side of Chicago than to navigate across a trackless desert? Does a narrowly specialized physician really possess and manage more knowledge than a traditional healer, who may know the medicinal uses of literally thousands of species and subspecies of herbs and plants?

This contemporary Western fragmentation manifests itself particularly in our view of the relationship between man and the rest of nature. The Western world-view sees man as apart from and opposed to nature, and nature as an opponent to be conquered and subdued. Contemporary science and technology foster and support this world-view, but its roots go back much further. It is a firmly entrenched part of Judeo-Christian tradition, based on Old Testament teachings and beliefs.

In this regard science and the Church, often regarded as adversaries, have a common cause. Both profit from a perception of nature as a hostile adversary, because both offer to shield and protect us. Both see themselves as buffers between man and nature, though of course in different ways. In *Where the Wasteland Ends,* Theodore Roszak traces the fragmentation of Western culture back through the development of science to early roots in our Judeo-Christian heritage.

The idea of a common cause between science and religion may seem startling, because we have been conditioned to think of them as in opposition. This common cause may be better seen when they are contrasted with a very different alternative, such as that presented by some of the older, more naturalistic religions and by alchemy.

Most people know of the witchcraft trials held during the Middle Ages, after which convicted witches were often hanged, drowned or burned at the stake. Unless you have a greater than average interest in the subject, you probably have the impression that these trials were uncommon, almost isolated events, totaling a few hundred or at most a few thousand incidents. Depending on whether your information comes from a scientific or religious perspective, you may think of the witches themselves as superstitious psychotics persecuted by their superstitious neurotic neighbors or as evil worshipers of the devil, holding black masses and casting evil spells on good God-fearing folk. Some probably fell into both these categories, perhaps even the thousands which most people think of as the number killed. But estimates of the total numbers of witches killed go much higher than that, into the millions during the sixteenth and seventeenth centuries. Many of these victims were members of naturalistic pagan religions which predated

Christianity and which were based on the idea of an essential harmony between man and nature.

What went on in the Middle Ages was not the persecution of a few isolated village loonies and devil worshipers by their superstitious neighbors. It was a *war*—a war between two opposing ways of seeing the world and our place in it. When the war was over, both parties in the winning coalition, science and the church, proceeded in their different ways to redefine the character of the opposition so that the real issues would be forgotten.

Another set of losers in this same war were the alchemists, whose objective was less the transmutation of lead into gold than the transmutation and perfection of their own internal natures. In addition to laboratory experimentation, the alchemists used chemical and metallurgical processes as a meditative focus and a way of aligning themselves with nature, in much the same way that some Zen adepts use archery or flower arranging. Many alchemical writings which superficially concern chemical processes, in fact, were also symbolic descriptions of internal processes and of the manipulation and combination of internal energies. That was certainly the case with Chinese Taoist alchemical writings.

The alchemists lost and have been depicted to succeeding generations as second rate pseudo-chemists trying to turn lead into gold. The view prevailed of man as separate and apart from nature, the "detached objective observer" who should conquer, subdue and exploit the natural world. Science and the Church each had their own turf, and Western society prospered. Lately, though, that view is being questioned. The fruits of science and technology are not all as sweet as they once seemed. Some, like pollution and the increasing amounts of carcinogens we are putting into the environment, are absolutely sour. These are the byproducts of reductionism, of seeing the world in fragmented pieces and ignoring the interconnections until they rise up and confront us.

We do seem to be moving toward a more holistic perception of ourselves and our place in the world. One of the ways this manifests itself is through the environmental movement and the concern for the ecology as a whole. It also manifests through the growing interest in meditative and other spiritual disciplines, and in rediscovering the wisdom of older, traditional societies.

Many of these societies have traditionally seen man as an integral part of the natural system, intertwined with the rest of life and the forces of nature in an interlocking, interconnected web. The gods, spirits and other deities they see in the world around them symbolize that interdependence. The ceremonies and prayers associated with activities like hunting, planting, or the coming of the rains serve to acknowledge and reinforce their awareness of it. Cultures which view man as an integral part of the natural system tend to develop the ability to coexist with that system on a long-term basis, neither destroying nor being destroyed by their environment.

In the contemporary Western world-view the material world is dominant. Life and consciousness are seen as byproducts of physical and chemical activity in the bodies which bear them, and the tendency is to assume that all things can be explained in material terms. No room exists in this world-view for disincarnate spirits or for magic.

Other cultures see much broader worlds, of which the material is but a part. They characterize these worlds in different ways, and sometimes it is difficult to tell what is meant to be taken literally and what symbolically. Some cultures, as a whole, or members of the cultures, probably think of spirits and deities of various kinds as real, while others use such entities as symbolic descriptions of aspects of the human psyche. This latter is the case, for example, of the talking animals in American Indian legends and of the demons described in *The Tibetan Book of the Dead.*

In the history of human thought, in a variety of different forms, the theme has arisen frequently that the material world itself is illusory—that it is belief in the material world, not the nonmaterial, which results from ignorance and superstition. Buddhist doctrine teaches that *samsara,* the world of birth and death, is an illusion resulting from our past conditioning. Plato's metaphor of the shadows on the wall of the cave seems to say the same thing, while Castaneda's mentor don Juan describes ordinary reality as "membership" in an "agreement" about how to perceive the world.

Some cultures provide methods of temporary escape from this illusion as a normal part of cultural life. The Senoi Indians believe that dreams are more real than the experiences of waking life, and have developed the practice of dreaming to an art over which they exercise considerable control. Australian aborigines have a state of consciousness called "dreamtime," in which they can know and do unusual things which they view as closer to reality than ordinary waking consciousness. Many other cultures use various forms of altered consciousness to contact reality more directly than in the waking state. The Western world-view, on the other hand, has tended to look askance at other states of consciousness and to label experiences in such states as "hallucinations."

Our Western scientific seekers of knowledge experience the same reality as everyone else. Their goal is simply to know it in greater detail. More traditional seekers of knowledge (the shamans, sorcerers and alchemists) have tried to know reality differently, to experience it in ways not immediately accessible to everyone.

The Western world-view admits no *magic*—real magic, that is, rather than sleight of hand. It assumes that everything has a material explanation, so that phenomena without such an explanation cannot exist. Belief in such phenomena, therefore, must result from ignorance and superstition. But if there is more, and we just fail to see it, then that argument falls apart. "Real magic" can exist, for those sensitive enough to perceive and manipulate the nonmaterial links of the world. Traditional cultures do practice magic—hunting magic, healing magic and other forms as well—as did the alchemists and the followers of Wicca. It works (and it does not always work) when the practitioner can become aware of and be aligned with the phenomenon she wants to affect in a way which allows this. Magic, like science, is a perceptual process, but with a very different character.

The magician is the perceptual antithesis of the scientist. The scientist tries to be the detached observer, separate from and not affecting the phenomenon he observes. The magician, on the other hand, is part of and at one with the phenomenon. She

knows it from the inside, and thus can affect its workings. This is
the essence of magic—not the chants, potions or other paraphernalia the magician happens to use to aid her. These outer
things play a role similar to that played by green gowns and
operating room jargon in surgery. Something is necessary as
part of the context surrounding the procedure, but its nature is
largely arbitrary. What really counts is the skill of the surgeon—
or the magician.

This illustrates another limiting characteristic of Western
perception—the tendency to take everything literally. We look
at the paraphernalia the shaman uses and at the obvious,
external aspects of her procedure. We see that those things, in
and of themselves, could not produce the results she seeks.
Thus, we conclude the results must be unattainable.

This is not to say that everything traditional peoples accept as
magic actually is magic. They do misunderstand some material
phenomena, and some medicine men and shamans are known to
use sleight of hand and illusion. But the fact that not everything
called *magic* is authentic does not mean no magic exists, any
more than the fact that the existence of Hollywood special
effects means that all space scenes are fake and man never
walked on the moon. Our tendency to take everything literally
distorts our understanding of the world-models of other
cultures. We look at their myths and legends, and we know the
world isn't like that in any literal sense. So we conclude they
are wrong. But traditional cultures, much more than we, know
that words only symbolize, even in the best of circumstances.
They make richer use of the symbolic character of language to
evoke deeper nonverbal understanding rather than to try to
verbally encapsulate literal truth.

In Hopi creation legends, the Hopi describe themselves as
originally coming up from "underneath." Taken literally, these
legends seem to claim that the Hopi originated in a world
beneath the ground, coming up through a hole in the surface of
the earth. In the light of what we know about the physical
characteristics of the earth, such a description sounds innane,
clearly the result of ignorance and superstition.

But those legends should not be taken literally. The Hopi
have a very sophisticated world model that cannot be fully

described in English without resorting to some fairly complex mathematics. They see basic, underlying reality as a hyperspace of more than three dimensions, and the world available to our senses as a three-dimensional hyperplane moving through that hyperspace. What we experience as complete objects are three-dimensional sections of entities with more than three dimensions. Things already existing in this larger hyperspace come into being in our world as the three-dimensional hyperplane reaches them. They remain while the hyperplane passes through them, and they disappear as the hyperplane leaves them and passes on.

To get a more concrete sense of this concept, imagine a two-dimensional plane sweeping across three-dimensional space. When the plane comes to a cube in space, a rectangle will appear. The rectangle will "exist" while the plane passes through the cube and will disappear when it passes beyond. A sphere in space will appear as a dot when the plane first contacts it, then as a disk whose size gradually increases to the diameter of the sphere, then decreases to a point again and disappears as the plane passes through and beyond the sphere. A more complex three-dimensional object will, of course, produce more complex two-dimensional sections as the plane passes through it.

From this kind of perspective, things seem to "bubble up" into existence as the hyperplane reaches them. A term like "underneath" seems appropriate to describe things which have not yet reached the surface of the hyperplane. The Hopi legends do not mean that the Hopi people originated beneath the ground in the three-dimensional world, but that they originated in a larger reality and "bubbled up" into this one. This world-view is reminiscent of that contained in the Chinese *Tao Te Ching*, where things are described as "manifesting out of the void."

One could argue about whether or not this description of reality is correct. It seems clear, though—and this is the point of interest here—that this is not the simple, unsophisticated and obviously false world-model that one might derive from a literal interpretation of the Hopi legends. Rather, it represents a highly sophisticated and complex world-view—as sophisticated as anything in our own cosmology. There is an obvious parallel between the Hopi world-view and Einstein's four-dimensional space-time. The difference, I think, is that Einsteinian space-time is simpler and less sophisticated. A mathematical characterization of the Hopi model would probably require many more dimensions. This should be expected, because Einstein was trying to explain a more limited set of phenomena—those associated with mass and movement—while the Hopis were concerned with the world as a whole. In keeping with the principles of science (discussed earlier), Einstein sought the most parsimonious explanation, and a simple four-dimensional space-time was enough.

The sophistication of other American Indian myths can be seen in the interpretations given to Plains Indian legends by Hyemeyohsts Storm in his book *Seven Arrows*. He discusses the structure of perception and the symbolic nature of legends, and interprets the various animal characters as aspects of the human psyche. The mouse, for example, represents human tendencies to see only what is just before our noses, and to gather things in (such as facts) and store them without giving any thought to the larger context.

The Western infatuation with the material world also reflects in the goals the culture sets for its members. We measure success primarily in material terms and use those standards to declare ourselves the most successful culture on earth. Other cultures prescribe different goals, often relating to personal growth and enlightenment. The accumulation of material possessions is seen as secondary, if not as an actual impediment to progress. Some judge that the Australian aborigines possess one of the richest spiritual and contemplative cultures on earth, yet they have almost no material possessions, and that culture seems to discourage their acquisition.

Typically in the West, we measure progress in terms of our ability to control, subjugate and exploit the natural world. Our science, technology and economy are all geared to those ends, and they usually reach them. We look at other cultures, measure them according to the same terms, and find them wanting. They would have developed technology if they could have, we think, because it is part of the natural order of things. They didn't, so we find them backward and primitive.

But if their goal were to live in harmony with nature rather than to exploit it, would they really need our kind of technology? What if they experience a richer world than we and want to grow in and expand their knowing of that world? Would more technology and more material goods help them? Not so long as what they have is sufficient (which it might not be after a period of contact with us). But can we really judge that we are superior because of our technology and material goods?

8

Health and Healing

The human body is a wondrous thing. Barring accidents and given reasonable treatment, it can sustain its owner in a healthy condition for a hundred years or more. Most last an average of 70 years, even with all the abuse we subject them to. Over that period, the body rebuilds itself a number of times. The body you now have is not the body you were born with, nor is it the body you will have when you die. The materials comprising it will have changed many times.

Things do go wrong. People get sick; organs malfunction and sometimes fail. The range of possible illnesses and malfunctions is great, perhaps limited only by the ability of health practitioners to identify and characterize those illnesses. And identify and characterize they do! Every human society has healers. Those healers, in turn, have theories and models of how the body works, of what kinds of things go wrong with it and why. These models provide the basis for diagnosis and treatment of illness by the practitioners who employ them.

The models vary tremendously. One tradition might see illness as possession by an evil spirit and treat it by a form of exorcism. Another might see the same illness as a blockage of the flow of life force and treat it by sticking pins into the patient to restore that flow. Yet a third might see it as the invasion of hostile beings and administer poisons to destroy the invaders. (This last is Western medicine. We call the invaders "microbes" and the poisons "antibiotics.") Yet despite their diversity and apparent incompatibility, all these healing traditions work, at least up to a point. Each seems capable of curing some illnesses and incapable of curing others; which is which varies from one tradition to another. No tradition, including Western medicine, shows a clear superiority across the spectrum of human illness.

All deal with the same basic entities, the human body and its healthy and unhealthy functioning, though sometimes from very different perspectives. Perhaps they all work because their perspectives are all valid, in spite of superficial differences, as will be discussed. Remember how different the same elephant can appear to a group of blind men.

Another reason they all work is that in some very real sense, none work. None of them really "cures." You create your own illnesses; only you can really cure them. An outside agent—drug, doctor or other healer—can aid in that process, can create conditions which make it easier to regain health; but the basic responsibility for cure lies with the patient. Some healing traditions see this more clearly than others and perhaps are the better for it.

A closer look at some of the similarities and differences between different healing traditions will help provide an integrating overview of some superficially incompatible perspectives. A few definitions may be worthwhile. By a *healing tradition* I mean a coherent body of thought and/or practice concerned with health, illness and healing. Western medicine is one such tradition, traditional Chinese medicine another. Both have large bodies of written, formalized knowledge associated with them. Other traditions, such as shamanism, may be based on formalized knowledge which does not exist in written form. Still others, such as faith healing and the laying-on-of-hands, may have almost no formalized knowledge but depend on the instincts and perceptions of the individual practitioner.

Health refers to the body's general state of functioning.

Health is relative; we have no absolute standards of health and no way of knowing how far what we generally consider "good health" lies below our real potential. *Illness* is a state having a clear negative impact on the individual's normal functioning. I won't try to define it more specifically because to do so would require adopting some particular healing tradition. To define it in terms of infection, for example, would be to see it from the Western medical perspective, while defining it in terms of c'hi flow would be to adopt the traditional Chinese perspective.

Healing is the process by which the body moves from illness to a more healthy natural condition. It may be aided in different ways; but it is something which takes place within the body, not something done to the body from outside. A *healer* is someone who functions to aid the process of healing. Depending on the tradition in which he works, he may be called a physician, chiropractor, shaman, acupuncturist, witch doctor or something else. *Diagnosis* is the process through which the healer identifies and classifies an illness according to his particular healing tradition, and *treatment* is what he does to alleviate the illness and aid the healing process.

The healing tradition you are likely to be most familiar with is contemporary *Western medicine* as commonly practiced today. Western medicine is *allopathic,* which means that it treats symptoms in a manner intended to produce the opposite effect. Fever, for example, is treated with drugs to reduce fever, such as aspirin. Many illnesses are viewed as resulting from the invasion of the body by hostile microorganisms (the "germ theory" of disease) and are classified according to the type of microorganism found or believed to be responsible. Others are seen as malfunctions of internal organs (e.g., heart or kidney disease) or of one of the body's self-regulatory processes (e.g., high blood pressure). In some cases the mechanism by which the body rebuilds itself may fail, resulting in cancer, an uncontrolled growth of abnormal tissue. Non-germ-caused illnesses are seen as resulting from factors such as diet, exposure to external toxic substances, chronic abuse of the body (e.g., stress and overwork) and genetic factors. Some cancers are viewed as having such causes, while others are thought to be caused by germs (viruses).

Germ-caused illnesses are frequently treated with drugs

intended to destroy the invading microorganisms. Non-germ-caused illnesses may be treated with drugs to counter symptoms produced by the illness (e.g., to reduce blood pressure) or by surgery to repair or remove the malfunctioning organ (e.g., cardiac surgery or hysterectomy). In cancer treatment, the abnormal tissue is thought of as an invader to be destroyed by X-rays or drugs, or removed surgically.

Traditional Chinese medicine works from a very different perspective. The body is viewed as a system of energy flows, rather than interconnected parts. The energy, called *c'hi*, is thought to move along pathways known as *meridians*. In healthy individuals this flow is smooth and balanced. Illness both results from and manifests itself as an imbalance in the flow, producing a deficit or an excess of c'hi somewhere in the body. The purpose of treatment is to correct this imbalance. This may be done by stimulating appropriate points on the meridians (the acupuncture points), using manual stimulation (acupressure), needles (acupuncture), or heat (moxibustion). It may also be done by rebalancing the system through the administration of herbs or herb teas.

The idea that health is related to some kind of energy which constantly flows through us sounds foreign to Western ears, and for that reason may strike you as strange and discomforting. It is an idea, however, which recurs in different forms in many cultures. The Chinese, as noted, call the energy *ch'i*. The Japanese call it *ki;* the Indian yogis call it *prana;* Hawaiians call it *mana;* and the !Kung call it *n'um*. Wilhelm Reich called it *orgone,* and the Russians, coming to it through parapsychological research rather than cultural tradition, call it *bioplasma.* In English it is sometimes called *vital force* or *life force,* and is probably the same energy we refer to as *nervous energy.*

As the names vary, so do the details of the characterization. The Chinese describe this energy as something internal, a part of you. You can develop more of it, learn to feel it and move it around, and use it to direct and move your body. Some cultures talk of it as the life force of the universe, something which flows through everything all the time, reminiscent of the ether which physicists once hypothesized as the medium through which light and other electromagnetic waves traveled. When you begin to feel it, according to these models, you are simply becoming aware of a flow that was there all the time.

If you would like to feel this energy, try the following exercise. Sit quietly, relax, and allow your body to still itself. Hold your hands in front of you, palms facing inward, about six inches apart—as if you were holding a large grapefruit, perhaps, or a small balloon. Keep your hands relaxed, and imagine energy flowing down your arms and into the space between your hands. Don't actively do anything to make it flow; just imagine it. Imagine the space between your hands filling up, turning into a vibrant, pulsating ball of energy.

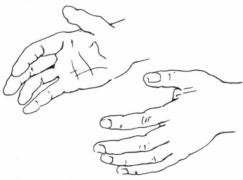

Soon you should begin to feel sensations in your hands. You may feel warmth, perhaps a tingling in the palms and fingertips. You may even find a finger or a thumb beginning to vibrate involuntarily. When you feel these sensations, begin to move your hands together very slightly, maybe a quarter of an inch or so. Move them as though the ball of ch'i you are holding were a balloon, and you just wanted to squeeze it enough to feel it push back against your hands.

And push back it will! You will feel a slight resistance to the movement of your hands, as if you were pushing against a very soft balloon, perhaps, or moving your hands through a viscous liquid.

You have just created a ball of ch'i. With practice, you can learn to make it stronger and to do it more easily. You can also make the ball a different size. The six inch ball is a good one to start with, but with practice you can make one a yard across, or create a flow between your thumb and forefinger. Later, we will examine other things to do with the flow.

It was this experience—actually, the variation we'll do next—that first opened me up to the existence of a much broader reality than the Western material world in which I lived at the time. This was the first big "crack" in my "cosmic egg," the one that opened up far enough for me to see that there was something on the other side. This chink stayed open so that I could go back to it and work on widening it when opportunities arose. It came at a time when I had been studying T'ai Chi for about a year. I was intellectually familiar with the concept of ch'i, but not really sure what to make of it. All of a sudden, there it was, an energy within me which I could make myself aware of and control.

"But wait," you might be saying. "All those sensations could just be from suggestion. That doesn't prove there's any such thing as ch'i." As far as proof goes, that's right. None of these exercises *proves* anything, they just provide a partial opening through which you have a chance to see something you haven't noticed before. But they can't make that happen, and they can't rule out other explanations for what you experience.

This exercise is particularly suspect the first time you try it. You've probably had similar sensations before, perhaps when your hand "fell asleep," and you don't need esoteric explanations for that. The sensations are subtle, just the kind that might be produced by suggestion. As you experience the ball more often, some of these doubts will weaken. Right now, though, they are very reasonable. I had the same doubts when I first experienced the ch'i. I knew that my mind was capable of producing such sensations, independent of whether or not I was really experiencing any such thing as ch'i. The thing I found convincing, though—the thing that really cracked my cosmic egg—was when I found that the ch'i could be transferred from one person to another. When someone else caused ch'i to flow, I could feel it, and when I caused it to flow, other people could feel it. That will be the next exercise.

For this exercise you will need a friend who has also made and felt a ball of ch'i. Have your friend create a ball, and when it is strong, pass your hand slowly through it from top to bottom in a slicing motion. You should be able to feel the difference as you pass into and out of the ball. It may feel warm, cool, tingly or just "funny," but you should sense some difference between being in the ball and out of it.

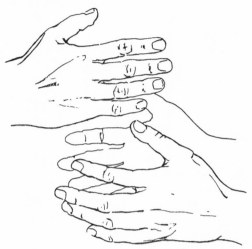

As a variation of this exercise, make a ball of ch'i of your own while your friend makes a larger one, enough larger to fit around yours. Place your hands, including your ball of ch'i, within your friend's larger ball. As you do, you should feel your ch'i more strongly, as both balls combine. Now reverse these execises, and let your friend feel your ch'i.

An obvious extension of this exercise suggests itself—closing your eyes and seeing if you can feel your friend's ch'i without looking. Go ahead and try it, but don't be too surprised if it doesn't work as well as with your eyes open. It becomes much harder to feel subtle phenomena such as these when you try to "test" them and to force yourself to decide intellectually whether or not they are "really there."

To see why this is true, recall the role of the ego in creating and maintaining your ongoing experiential reality. The ego filters and selects from the mass of information and sensation available, blocking out most of it and allowing only that which supports your current experiential reality to enter conscious-

ness. The sensation of the ch'i has been there all the time
—all your life, in fact—but your ego never let it slip through
to consciousness before. The exercise gave you a way to amplify
the sensation and bring it to consciousness without challenging
the ego process directly. The ego allowed the sensation and
only put up minor resistance in the form of doubts that you were
experiencing anything beyond ordinary "suggestion."

When you try to test the experience, to see if you can feel the
ch'i with your eyes closed, you are presenting the ego with a
far more direct and threatening challenge. Your ego maintains a
reality in which that sort of information is not available for use in
conscious decision making. And now here you are, asking for
just that. You may be able to do it, but don't be surprised if you
can't, at least not without further training in relaxing the
constraints your ego places on the reality you experience.

This has been somewhat of a diversion, but a useful one.
Having experienced the ch'i, and having begun to learn to make
it flow, you are in a better position to understand non-Western
healing traditions. You can see healing from more than one
perspective now, and as a result, can develop a fuller understanding of the overall process.

Is disease caused by the germs of Western medicine or the
bad ch'i flow of the Chinese? I believe that both views are
correct, and the apparent incompatabilities between the two
are largely illusory. Any difficulty we have in seeing that results
from interpreting the concept of *cause* too narrowly, from
trying to structure the world so that each cause produces a
well-defined effect, and each effect has only one cause. The
world just isn't that way.

Though the Western medical model does not recognize it,
there is an energy flow through the body. When you are healthy,
that flow is smooth and balanced and your body is in harmony.
Hostile "germs" do live in your body but in small numbers kept
in check by your natural defense mechanisms. Your "resistance"
is high, we say. Tiredness, cold, trauma or other stress may
disrupt and unbalance this flow, making your "resistance" drop.
Germs can then multiply, taking advantage of your inability to
keep them in check. This further disrupts the balance, allowing
the invading germ colony to grow. You now feel sick, with

whatever symptoms your particular combination of imbalances produces. You have a large colony of invading germs in your body, your ch'i flow is disrupted, and the balance and harmony characteristic of good health are gone.

What caused the illness—the imbalanced ch'i flow or the germs? Which came first, the chicken or the egg? In either case, the two are intertwined in a mutually reinforcing cycle. The germs were able to multiply because of an imbalance in the flow, and magnified that imbalance as they did so. The germs now maintain the imbalance, and they exist only because of the imbalance. The disease may be treated by attacking and breaking the cycle from either side. Attack the germ colony, as Western medicine does, and the colony may be weakened enough to allow the body to reassert and rebalance itself. Rebalance the ch'i flow, as Chinese medicine does, and the now stronger body will be able to cope with the invading germs. The apparent either/or choice between the two models is fallacious, like the choice between the 13 and the B.

There are many healing traditions based on concepts of balance and energy flow, though the details of the model and the methods used to rebalance the body vary widely. Some use herbs and similar remedies, while others use dance or other forms of movement. Among the !Kung, for example, the healing energy is called n'um, and healing takes place during cere-monial dances which cause the n'um to flow. Similar balancing mechanisms may be operative in healing traditions which conceptualize illness in terms of possession by evil spirits and healing as a form of exorcism or divine intervention. The "laying-on-of-hands" is another way of accomplishing the same thing.

One of the reasons some of these systems look so much like superstitious mumbo jumbo to many Westerners is that they involve no material contact between healer and patient, at least none that we recognize as of therapeutic value. But that does not negate them. The energies involved can be detected, amplified, and directed by the mind, as you saw from the last exercises.

In fact, the kind of flow you learned how to induce in those exercises can be used for healing purposes. It is good for sprains and stiff muscles and can also provide some relief from sore throat, menstrual cramps and clogged sinuses. If you want to try it, the next time you have a sick friend, proceed as follows.

Have your friend lie down in a comfortable place, and seat yourself where you can easily reach the affected area. Place your hand on or over the area, as you prefer. (This may be done with or without clothing, and physical contact is not necessary. The best guide is what you feel comfortable with.) Flow your ch'i out through your arm and into your friend, just as you would if you were making the ball. Transmit calmness and relaxation along with your ch'i. Don't worry about getting exactly the right place; the ch'i seems to flow where it is needed even if the placement of your hand is slightly off.

As the ch'i flows, your friend will probably begin to feel warmth and perhaps tingling in the affected area. The soreness, irritation or discomfort should diminish. Continue as long as you feel comfortable giving and your friend feels comfortable receiving. Five to ten minutes at a stretch is usually good. One word of caution—if your friend feels uncomfortable, quit. You're not helping. Sometimes, in the head especially, the extra ch'i will be felt as an uncomfortable pressure, and if continued can cause a headache.

Don't expect any miracles from this technique and you won't be disappointed. It can provide temporary relief and promote healing, but it is not likely to produce instant cures. It should be in addition to, not in place of, any other form of treatment normally used. As you do more of it, you will get better at it.

ILLNESS AS A WITHDRAWAL OF AWARENESS

We will now consider illness from a somewhat different point of view—as a withdrawal of awareness and energy (or ch'i) from the affected area—with healing as a return of awareness and energy flow. By *awareness* here I don't mean our waking conscious awareness, but a kind of generalized self-awareness that often lies below the level of consciousness and provides an organizing field for our activity as living beings. This generalized awareness is closely associated with, if not actually the same as, what Eastern traditions describe as the free flow of energy. This particular characterization of illness and healing is my own, though it does have parallels with Wilhelm Reich's "body armor" and the ideas about self-image which Moshe Feldenkrais discusses in *Awareness through Movement.*

Remember the "contraction reaction" you saw in Chapter 5, locking your arm in place at the moment you encounter a "solid" object. We looked at that contraction as a gross muscular reaction to gross physical contact. It also occurs on much finer levels, down to the cellular level and possibly below, and it occurs in reaction to non-physical as well as physical contact. The sudden tightening when you feel threatened (as in the exercise on broad and narrow awareness we did in Chapter 3, for example) is a contraction reaction. A contraction reaction also occurs, though more subtly, in response to soft, pleasurable contacts, such as stroking a pet or the touch of a lover.

The contraction reaction serves to define the boundary between each of us and the rest of the world, to maintain us as separate entities in accordance with the ego's concept of reality. It creates a barrier between us and the things we come in contact with, protecting us against too much intrusion by those things into our space. This barrier acts to impede the free flow of ch'i through the body, while the absence of contraction enhances and promotes that flow. The more relaxed we are, then, the more freely the ch'i can flow.

This does not mean that relaxation and ch'i flow are necessarily the same; they are not. Relaxation without ch'i flow is the kind of flaccid immobility people often associate with the term *relaxation.* Relaxation with ch'i flow is a strong healthy state we approach at times to varying degrees. Few of us, though, ever get anywhere near really good health in those terms.

The few who do include the real "masters" in disciplines like Zen, T'ai Chi and the Sufi traditions. They live healthy and illness-free lives, are quick and fluid in their movements even in old age, and are capable of almost superhuman feats of strength. In *Zen and the Art of Archery,* Eugene Herrigel describes the ability of his Zen teacher to hold a powerful Japanese hunting bow at full draw with his arms completely relaxed, without apparent strain or tension. Even moderately competent practitioners of internal martial arts like T'ai Chi and Aikido can sit or stand in a relaxed manner in spite of the best efforts of several strong men to push them over.

You can experience this kind of relaxed power through an Aikido exercise often called "the unbendable arm." *Find a friend again, preferably one reasonably well matched to you in size and strength. Stand facing each other, about an arms length apart. Straighten your right arm and rest the lower edge of your right wrist on your friend's left shoulder. Your friend should lock his hands over your elbow and apply a steady downward pull. Resist this pull and attempt to keep your arm straight while your friend gradually increases his pull until you can no longer resist and your arm collapses.*

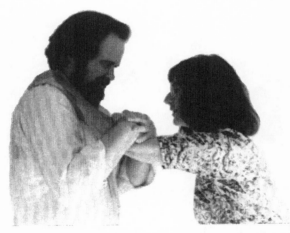

Observe what happens during that process; notice how your arm responds to the pull. You put increasing effort into resisting your friend's pull, and your arm suddenly collapses when the effort becomes too great. Your attention focuses on the point of contact between your arm and your friend's hands—the point of conflict. This is how we usually respond to the world, using contraction to separate ourselves from and defend against external disturbances.

Try it again, but do it differently. Rest your hand on your friend's shoulder as before. Let your hand, arm, shoulder and entire body relax. Extend your fingers and flow ch'i through your arm and out your fingers, as you did when you made the ball of ch'i. Think of your ch'i as water and your arm as a hose, and imagine water flowing through your arm and spraying out through your hand.

Once you have that flow going, your friend should again try to pull down your arm. He should pull down gently and increase his pull gradually so that you can retain the feeling of flowing. A sudden sharp pull might distract you and shift you back to the contraction response, and that's not what this exercise is about. You will notice his hands on your arm and his downward pull, but don't shift your attention to them. Make no attempt to actively resist. Just keep your attention on the flow, even if your arm starts to bend.

Your friend will find that it takes considerable pressure to bend your arm, if it bends at all. You will be aware of his effort, though less conscious of the amount of energy he is expending than you were the first time. If your arm does bend, it will bend slowly and gradually without the sudden collapse you experienced the first time. Even then, you may be able to straighten it again without muscular effort, by strengthening the flow through your arms and imagining the way a high pressure flow

stiffens a water hose.

This exercise provides you with the experience of two very different ways of interacting with the world. The first, which we use most of the time, consists of contracting and pushing back. The second involves a relaxed and balanced acceptance of the world, flowing with rather than fighting against it. We all do this sometimes too, though not as often as we could.

When things go well we tend to attribute our experience to external forces—to luck or the people we happen to come in contact with. We might feel that "Everyone I met today seemed so pleasant." Similarly, we blame the external world when things go poorly. "People really seemed crabby today," we complain. We see the world as pushing and forcing us to push back, rather than simply responding to our push. It is a matter of perception again, of two different ways of bringing things into focus. It's like the faces and vase or the B and 13.

Which way we see things can have important consequences. If we see the sources of our conflicts as external (e.g., your friend's downward pull in the exercise), then the only ways we have of responding are to contract and fight back (as you did the first time) or to give in and be dominated (as you did when your arm collapsed). If we recognize the source of conflict as being in ourselves, however, we may see that we each have the power to avoid creating conflict. We can flow with the world, immune to disturbance by outside forces (as when you made your "unbendable arm"). This is as true of the psychological, emotional and verbal conflicts we face every day as it is of physical conflict.

In an exercise like this one, or the exercise in Chapter 5 involving getting up out of a chair, the choice between pushing and flowing is relatively clear. In many of the conflicts occurring in our daily lives—clashes with lovers or coworkers, or even an exchange of dirty looks with another driver over the right-of-way—the choice may be harder to see, at least at the time of the conflict. We respond "automatically" without thinking, without realizing we have a choice, though we may be able to see it in retrospect. In the situations most affecting our health, the choices may be made so far below the level of consciousness that we may never be aware of them at all, even in retrospect.

But the choices are always there; we make them, and we live with their consequences.

The kinds of choices we make as part of our disease processes became clear to me a few years ago, when I spent a week in bed with a "virus sore throat." I had a fairly high fever and a very painful sore throat. I was "treating" myself by staying as relaxed as possible in order to let my body devote all its energy to healing, and by consciously directing ch'i to my throat from time to time to promote the healing process.

After a while, I became aware that I was contracting and tightening my throat, at a submuscular and perhaps even a cellular level, and that I had been doing this all the time my throat was sore. At this time I was beginning to understand the role that the contraction reaction played in the perception of "solidity"; but I had not yet been aware of it on this level, so this was a new insight to me.

As I became aware that *I* was the cause of the contraction, I realized that *I* could inhibit the contraction and relax. I could only do it a bit at a time—almost cell by cell, it felt like. But by keeping my attention on it for more than an hour, I was able to relax my entire throat. When I was finished, my throat felt fine; it was no longer sore at all! The soreness was the product of the contraction, and when I let go of the contraction, the soreness disappeared.

I congratulated myself on having cured my sore throat and turned my attention elsewhere. As soon as I did that, it seems the conditioned responses that had given me the sore throat in the first place took over. Within a few minutes my sore throat was back, as painful as it had ever been. I was in bed for several more days. I could get rid of the soreness any time I wanted to by devoting my full attention to my throat for an hour or so. But it would stay "cured" only while I kept my attention on it; otherwise I would unconsciously tighten up and bring the soreness back. It wasn't a very practical "cure," but it did give me some valuable insights into the nature of the disease process.

The contraction response is defensive. It serves as a barrier, a firebreak between us and some disturbance or source of conflict. The disturbance may be a friend pulling down on an arm, as in the last exercise, or it may be germs attempting to establish a colony in the throat. It may be a honking horn in traffic, a boss who yells at us for being late to work, or a client we fear may take his business elsewhere. The process, in all these cases, is much the same.

We respond to the disturbance by contracting, setting up a barrier between ourselves and the disturbance in order to wall it off. We don't set this barrier up at the physical boundary but further back, somewhere that seems more defensible. In effect, we give up some awareness and control of the area outside the barrier in order to consolidate at a stronger position.

If the disturbance is weaker than the barrier we erected, we will win. If not, the disturbance may threaten to overwhelm the barrier. We must fall back further, contract more, and create additional barriers between ourselves and the disturbance. In the end, either we contain it or it overwhelms us.

Let's watch that happen in the context of the last exercise. *Rest your arm on your friend's shoulder again, and don't flow your ch'i. As he gradually increases his pull down on your arm, resist his pull and watch how your resistance develops.*

Begin by noticing what happens as your friend reaches up and puts his hands on your arm. You should observe a slight contraction in your arm under his hand, establishing the boundary between your arm and his hand. It is the same kind of contraction you saw in the exercise in Chapter 5 involving grasping the wrist. You may also notice slight contractions in your wrist, shoulder and elbow, serving to make them rigid and define their place in space. This is your initial response. If your friend simply rests his hand on your arm, that will be enough to defend you against that disturbance and no further response will be necessary.

Your friend should slowly increase his downward pull. Your initial response will now prove insufficient. You must either give in and let him move your arm or strengthen and reinforce the barrier. Notice the process of falling back to a new position. As you make your arm rigid in response to the pull, you are not really fighting the pull with your arm. Rather, you allow your friend to pull on the arm as he will and fight back with your shoulder.

Additional contraction in your wrist, elbow and shoulder will help to keep your arm rigid, but eventually contraction will be needed in your wrist, hips, legs and feet so you can push back from the floor. Depending on how hard he pulls, you may stabilize your barrier and contain him, or his pull may prove too much and your arm will collapse.

The "geography" of the response is fairly clear in this case. It begins at the boundary between you and the initial disturbance (your friend's hand) and spreads to include areas threatened by the disturbance as it grows. The joints, for example, are threatened by the pull because it might force them to move. In the case of less well-defined disturbances, the "geography" might be harder to find. We respond to the beginnings of illness by trying to wall off and enclose the illness within our bodies, and against non-specific threats (like a yelling boss or the fear of losing a client) by a generalized contraction, stronger in some areas than others because of our particular, personal response patterns.

It's akin to the idea of using fortified settlements as a defense against marauding invaders, like the forts of the old West or the "strategic hamlet" program during the Viet Nam War. Move in behind defensible lines, temporarily relinquishing control of the territory beyond the lines to the enemy. And like fortified settlements, sometimes it works and sometimes it doesn't. The nature of the "enemy" may be such that the territory you gave up provides him a fertile ground in which to multiply and grow stronger, forcing you to fall back still further, giving him more room to grow. This seems to be what happens in the spread of infection and possibly in the case of some cancers as well.

When we contract and relinquish control of the "territory" beyond the contraction barrier, we open up that territory to invasion by any disturbance that finds fertile ground there, not just the disturbance against which the barriers were initially erected. The barriers we erect against discomfort when cold, wet or hungry thus also make us more susceptible to illness and infection. We usually describe this by saying that our "resistance" is lower.

Chronic barriers, maintained and reinforced over long periods and never completely relaxed, make the area of the body thus isolated particularly susceptible to illness. This accounts, I believe, for the association of certain illnesses with particular behavior patterns. Much has been written, for example, about the relationship between heart disease and the continued maintenance of high levels of stress, as in the stereotype of the hard-driving business executive. (Sometimes this is referred to as "type A" behavior.) Some cancer specialists have noted a higher incidence of cancer among people with repressed anger and resentment.

Cancer, in fact, seems a particularly likely disease to be brought about in this way. It represents a basic failure of the mechanisms by which the body maintains and rebuilds itself. The loss of direction and control (the withdrawal of ch'i) brought about by the mind's withdrawal from the affected area provides a plausible explanation for that failure.

Cancer cells are always present in the body, the result of occasional errors occurring in the course of normal body maintenance. Ordinarily, these cells do not reproduce in significant numbers, and their presence goes largely unnoticed. Cancer results when these cells begin to reproduce uncontrollably, squeezing out and replacing normal tissue. The reasons this occurs are not well understood, but some sort of failure of the body's immune system is thought to be involved.

From the perspective under consideration here, the following explanation suggests itself. The body is not the simple, basically mechanical system the Western medical model considers it to be. The mind—perhaps in the form of some "life force," the ch'i or a generalized form of awareness—permeates the healthy body and provides the template into which the body fits itself. This generalized awareness gives overall direction and management to the body, including the processes of cell division and reproduction. It encourages the reproduction of normal cells as required by the body's ongoing needs, and discourages the survival and reproduction of abnormal cells.

When we contract, we withdraw awareness from the areas beyond the barrier and leave them without control, or at least with lessened control. This increases the likelihood of abnormal cell growth. So long as the uncontrolled periods are short and intermittent, we can easily reassert control when we stop contracting and remove the barriers. If the absence becomes chronic, however, abnormal growth may develop to the point where this is not possible. We then fall back and create new barriers against the abnormal tissue, opening up greater areas where it can grow and flourish. The cancerous cycle has begun.

It's a little like keeping a garden. No matter what you plant, some weeds are likely to find their way in. As long as you tend the garden regularly, you get the weeds while they are small and it's relatively easy to keep the garden weed-free. If you leave the garden alone too long, however, the weeds will have a chance to grow and flourish. Eventually, they will take over and force out the other plants.

This explanation of cancer does not deny the importance of factors frequently cited as causes of it, such as carcinogenic substances like asbestos or cigarette smoke, viruses, or psychological patterns of repressed anger. Rather, it may suggest a comprehensive explanation of how these other causes work. They act as particularized irritants inviting localized contraction reactions, thus creating localized "strongholds" where cancer can develop. Cigarette smoke, for example, continually irritates the surface of the lungs and leads to the erection of a chronic contraction barrier there. This results in withdrawal of awareness and control (ch'i), and allows the development of lung cancer.

If this explanation is correct and cancer does result from a loss of control accompanying a withdrawal of awareness from the part of the body where the cancer grows, then that process should be reversible. It should be possible to arrest and perhaps even cure cancer by reestablishing awareness and allowing the body's normal regulatory mechanisms to take control again. Treatment programs exist whose success seems explainable in these terms. The best known of these, perhaps, is the program developed by Dr. Carl Simonton, a Texas radiologist and author of *Getting Well Again.*

The principal technique Simonton uses is visualization, used as a form of treatment in its own right in conjunction with other forms of therapy. He asks the patient to visualize his cancer, in whatever symbolic form is comfortable, and to visualize his treatment as successfully attacking and destroying the cancer. The particular form this imagery takes is unimportant. Clinically valid imagery, in particular, is not necessary. One successful patient saw his cancer as a large hamburger-like mass and his treatment as ravenous dogs tearing chunks off the mass and devouring it.

This sort of treatment is not something the healer *does to* the patient, like surgery or radiation therapy. It is something the patient *does for* himself, with the advice and guidance of the healer. For it to work, the patient must accept responsibility for his own health and must be willing to commit the necessary time and energy. Simonton has found that the patients who were helped were those who devoted themselves wholeheartedly to the task with a positive attitude, while those who did it sporadically and halfheartedly usually did not improve.

The patient must also be willing to take the necessary responsibility and to see himself as capable of reexerting control. One patient who was not helped saw his cancer as a pack of large rats and his attack on that cancer as little yellow pills dropped along the paths the rats used. When a rat ate one of the pills it would sicken, but would usually recover and be meaner and stronger than ever. The patient died of his cancer.

Let's also briefly examine *faith healing* and see how it looks from the perspective outlined here. Faith healers do treat cancer, and claims of success are made. The late Katherine Kuhlman, in particular, is said to have cured patients with cancers in advanced stages. Patients have reportedly come to her in wheelchairs or even hospital beds, too pain-wracked to move, then gotten up and walked from the auditorium after receiving the "power of the Lord" from her. Skeptical investigators who have followed up on these reports acknowledge them to be true, but claim that many "cured" patients shortly suffered relapses and returned to their original condition or worse.

Both the initial "cure" and the following relapse are compatible with the model outlined here. The faith healer relaxes the contraction barriers the patient has erected, thus effecting a temporary "cure." But this does nothing to remove the disturbance against which those barriers were erected, nor does it alter the response patterns that caused the patient to erect those barriers in the first place. The patient goes home, feeling no personal responsibility for either the illness or the subsequent cure, and does nothing to remove the disturbance before he walls himself off from it again. The response patterns reassert themselves, and soon he's right back where he started.

Part of that argument deserves a bit more attention, and perhaps an exercise for clarification. By relaxing the patient's contraction barriers, the healer apparently effected a temporary "cure" without affecting the disturbance against which the barriers were erected. In advanced cancer patients, that disturbance might consist of a large tumor mass. Thus I'm suggesting, though I certainly don't know for sure, that some of the patients treated by Katherine Kuhlman and other faith healers have felt cured and been mobile and free of pain, in spite of the physical presence of the tumors that they thought were causing their earlier pain and immobility.

The reason for this apparent contradiction lies in the fact, I think, that we attribute the effects of our illnesses to the wrong cause. I am suggesting that pain, limited mobility and the other restrictions we feel when we are ill seldom result directly from the disturbance to which we attribute them. Rather, they are produced by the barriers we erect to separate ourselves from the disturbance. We set up defenses to protect ourselves, and those defenses limit and constrain us. If we let go of the defenses, most of the constraints will disappear.

This is the same lesson we saw in a different context in some of the earlier exercises, such as the exercise in Chapter 1 involving trying to raise your arm. When you encounter what your ego believes to be a threatening external object, you contract and make yourself rigid to keep the object out of your "space." This rigidity makes you unable to move, and you attribute your immobility to the external object.

Contraction is the ego's response to what is perceived as a threat, the ego's way of walling you off from and defending against the threat. If the disturbance persists in spite of that contraction, the ego may order further contraction, even when that contraction itself is worse than the threat.

Pain is the body's way of saying "Enough!"

Pain is the way the body responds when the contraction

itself becomes potentially damaging. It is a response to the contraction, not the disturbance; it is trying to tell you to do something else instead. When the contraction is relaxed, the pain will often disappear. That's what happened to the pain of my sore throat when I saw what was happening and allowed my throat to relax. But the ego habitually responds in the wrong way, contracting further to defend against the pain. This creates a cycle of contraction-pain-contraction which may continue to create pain long after the disturbance against which the contraction was originally erected has disappeared.

Perhaps we can clarify that with an exercise. Unlike the previous exercises, this one will involve a little pain. Properly used, pain can be a marvelous aid to learning. It may be, in fact, that no real learning can take place without pain, even if only the psychological pain of letting go of old beliefs and opening up to new possibilities.

Find a friend again. This time you'll need a friend you trust, someone you know will apply force gradually and stop when you say. Your friend should slowly and steadily twist your arm, gradually increasing the pressure. As he does so, adopt an attitude of knowing that it's going to hurt, and of protecting yourself against that hurt. Resist slightly, though not enough to prevent him from twisting your arm. Notice the gradual increase in both the contraction and the pain, and when the pain reaches some moderate level, tell your friend to stop and hold it where it is.

As your friend holds your arm in place, continue to resist him and to be aware of the pain in your arm. Notice how far your arm went and how much it hurts in that position. Now change your attitude. Realize that your friend isn't twisting your arm anymore; he's just holding it still. You don't need to keep fighting him to keep him from twisting it further. You can relax, without changing the position of your arm, and just be where you are. As you do so, the pain will disappear. You will discover it wasn't the twisting of your arm that caused the pain, it was your resistance to that twist.

When your arm is twisted, the twist stretches the muscles of your arm, and when they stretch further than they like to go, they hurt. The source of the pain, then, is your overstretched muscles.

The reason your muscles feel stretched is that they're contracting as hard as they can to keep your arm from being twisted further. They aren't stretched to their limit, because if they were they wouldn't be able to contract. So if they weren't contracting, they would be longer, and they wouldn't feel stretched. The pain comes from the tightness in your muscles, to be sure. But the source of that tightness is the fact that they are overcontracted, not the external twist. If you simply relax the muscles, without changing position at all, the muscle fibers will elongate and loosen, and the pain will disappear.

That is often easier said than done. Even when you realized your friend was only holding your arm and not really twisting it, you may have found it difficult to relax and let the pain go away. And when you think the twist will be applied harder if you do relax, it can be nearly impossible.

That's because of our old friend the ego and its habit of predicting and controlling. The ego senses the twist already on your arm and predicts that unless you resist your arm will be twisted even more. Your ego also believes that the twist is producing the pain and that allowing any more twist will produce more pain. Your ego orders your arm to contract to prevent further twisting. This contraction—your reaction to the twist rather than the twist itself—causes the pain you feel.

Try the following variation of the last exercise. Have your friend slowly twist your arm again, but this time don't resist. Let yourself go in a relaxed and passive manner, and just observe your arm being twisted. Stop your friend when you reach the same level of pain as before, and compare the position of your arm with what it was last time.

It probably went much further before you stopped it. It stopped for the same reason this time: your ego predicted that it would hurt to allow it to go further, so it ordered the muscles to contract and stop the arm. But that didn't happen as soon when you relaxed and observed the process.

Try the exercise again. This time, don't just relax while your friend twists your arm; think that you want to twist it. You want to see how far it will go, and your friend is helping you to explore the limits of your range of motion. Again, stop when you feel the same level of pain, and see how the position this time compares with the two previous times.

Your arm should have gone farther still. Look at its position this time, and ask yourself how you would have predicted that position would feel at the time you did the first version of the exercise.

Intention matters! In each case, your arm stopped twisting when your ego decided it had gone far enough and stopped it. But notice how much farther you went the third time, when you took a positive attitude toward the twist and saw it as something you wanted to do, than you did the first time, when you saw it as something being forced on you and resisted. Who knows, maybe there's a general principle of some sort there.

Think about what it has to say about exercise, in particular. Competent instructors in disciplines like yoga, T'ai Chi and the Feldenkrais Method constantly stress relaxation and movement without excessive contraction. Move without effort or strain, they say. Go to the limit of your ability to move loosely, but not past it. With practice, that limit will move, further and faster than it would with a lot of stretching, effort and pain.

HEALING MODELS AND LARGER WORLD-VIEWS

Health and healing are not distinct activities split off and isolated from the rest of life; they are part of its total fabric. Healing traditions and the models of health on which they rest reflect the larger world-views from which they spring. Let us consider briefly this interconnection as it relates to some of the various healing models discussed.

Western medicine reflects the fundamental separation of man and nature so basic to the Western world-view—with nature (in this case, illness) an enemy to be conquered. Practitioners of Western medicine like to think of it as a science and so emphasize the particular form of this separation so stressed by science—separation between the scientific observer (the physician) and the object of his observation (the patient and his illness).

In keeping with the prevalent scientific penchant for seeing the world in mechanistic terms, Western medicine sees the body as a complex machine. Illness is a malfunction of that machine, to be repaired, or perhaps an enemy bent on damaging the machine, to be fought and overcome. Treatment is something the physician does *to* the patient, or more precisely, to the patient's body. In the struggle between the physician and the illness, the patient is only a bystander.

Treatments such as that developed by Dr. Simonton are exemplary of a new approach to healing which seems to be gathering momentum in this country. Sometimes called "holistic medicine," this eclectic approach attempts to learn from a variety of healing traditions and other sources, combining the best from each. One of its main characteristics is a strong emphasis on the personal responsibility each individual bears for his or her own health.

The energy flows in the body responsible for health and healing in the traditional Chinese model are extensions and reflections of the flows the Chinese see in the universe—the balance between yin and yang, hard and soft. The world within is the microcosm, reflecting the complexity and the variation of the external macrocosm. World-views which place considerable importance on the role of deities or other spirits in the workings of the world tend to give those deities a central place in the healing process. This is true, for example, of the !Kung healing model or of faith healers like Katherine Kuhlman. My own model of health in terms of awareness and the contraction response is likewise a product of the wider world-view from which it stems. In this case the principle roots were an interest in movement and the martial arts, and a focus on perception and awareness as integrating concepts.

The phenomena of health and healing are too rich and complex to be fully captured in a single conceptual model, be it the Western medical model, the traditional Chinese, or any of the others touched on here. This does not mean that any of these models is wrong, but only that they are all incomplete. Each emphasizes some parts of the phenomena and deemphasizes others, with that selection strongly influenced by the large context within which the model develops. If we understand this, we can draw from each when it is useful and avoid getting stuck in any single one.

9

Magic
and Extrasensory Perception

Magic and extrasensory perception have a significant relationship to perception in general. For this discussion, the term *ESP* describes knowing and perceiving the world other than through the ordinary senses, while *magic* refers to phenomena in which the mind produces effects in the world without direct material causation.

ESP thus includes phenomena like telepathy, clairvoyance and precognition; while magic encompasses phenomena such as hunting-magic, firewalking and levitation. This distinction turns out to be somewhat artificial, because the distinction between perception of and interaction with the world is itself artificial. Nonetheless, it is convenient for purposes of discussion.

I will take for granted that ESP and magic happen. Some fakery does exist, to be sure, but so does real magic. If you are uncomfortable with that assumption, grant it hypothetically, for the sake of the argument, and see if my explanations make sense. The really amazing thing, it turns out, is not the existence of phenomena like magic and ESP. Rather, it is the way we blind ourselves to and deny them, all the while using them to

161

create and maintain the illusion that we live in a world where they do not exist.

The contemporary Western positivist world-view sees mind as the by-product of electrical and chemical activity in the brain, and believes the senses to be the mind's only sources of information about the outside world. That view is seriously flawed. Enormous amounts of information about the world "out there" are at least potentially available directly, not through the senses. It may be that you can know almost anything, anytime, if you just understood how and where to look. What limits you are your abilities to process information—to digest and understand it—not the amount of raw data available.

How could this be? Where could the information come from, and how could you get it? If you believe that you are "nothing but" a physical entity with the senses providing your only channels to the outside world, these things seem impossible. If you allow the possibility that you are more, however, the situation changes. Even without answering those questions, you can begin to get a partial sense of where the answers lie and to understand the larger reality of which you are only dimly aware.

One conceptualization of what that "more" might be, which appears in various forms in a wide variety of esoteric teachings, involves the idea that the "you" of which you are conscious is only part of a larger "you" with broader and more universal awareness. In such a conceptualization your mind is not simply the byproduct of electrical and chemical activity in your brain, but a nonmaterial entity existing independently of your body and brain. Your mind uses your body and brain and spends a lot of time there, to be sure. But that's out of choice (albeit conditioned and involuntary choice, but choice nonetheless) and not necessity. It can be elsewhere and know other things.

As a more concrete metaphor for this sort of concept, think of life as a *game*—perhaps as a board game, like *Monopoly*. The world is the playing area—the board—and we are the pieces. You are a piece, a counter in the game like one of the little colored counters in *Monopoly*. The actions you can take and the information you can have available on which to base those actions are limited by the rules under which you play.

Generally, you can be aware only of your immediate area of the board, as your senses show it to you, and your actions are limited by what you perceive in that way.

But in a larger sense, you are not just the piece on the board. You are also the player, sitting above the board and looking down at the whole game. As the player, you can know anything, because you can see the whole game. The rules prevent you as player from transmitting that knowledge to you as the piece. The ego is the filter which enforces these rules and keeps you, the piece, in your proper state of ignorance.

In *The Ultimate Athlete*, George Leonard presents a very readable discussion of this metaphor in more depth than I will go into here. A different characterization of the same core idea, that we are smaller parts of larger selves, can be found in the writings of Seth, the "disincarnate entity" who speaks through medium Jane Roberts (e.g., *Seth Speaks* and *The Nature of Personal Reality*). Seth claims we are fragments of larger multidimensional personalities, separate and independent while alive but reintegrating with those larger personalities when we die.

A different perspective on our larger connection with the universe, or perhaps simply a different variation on the same theme, sees us as all part of the same larger self. This idea frequently finds expression in the metaphor of a river, as in the lyrics from Peter Yarrow's song *River of Jordan*:

> There is only one river,
> there is only one sea,
> and it flows through you,
> and it flows through me.*

Think of yourself, your independent personality, as a cup of water scooped from the river, separate for a time but eventually merging again with the rest of the river. But even while separate, you remain connected to the river and can sense and appreciate that connection. Psychic Edgar Cayce felt he could dip back into the river when he needed to, and saw the river as the source for the information he received while in trance.

---

*Reprinted by permission of the author.

The image of a river as symbolic of all life also appears in American Indian mythology, among other places. The idea that life is tied into some kind of universal flow can also be found in Jung's idea of a "Collective Unconscious," the Japanese concept of "ki" as a universal life force, the Tao as the source from which all things are produced and to which all return.

Another variation on the theme that everything is inter-connected can be found in the Chinese ideas of *macrocosm* and *microcosm.* The world within is the microcosm, the world outside the macrocosm. The boundary between them is like a mirror; anything that happens on one side is reflected on the other. When a sparrow falls it does affect you, though you may not notice the effect. And changes in you do produce changes in the world around you, though they may be subtle and difficult to discern. Carl Pribram's description of the universe as a hologram provides a modern technological metaphor for the same basic concept.

When we come across concepts like these, we often get hung up on their particular verbal characterizations. We look for inconsistencies and differences among them, for ways in which they appear to contradict one another. We want to accept one and reject the others, or reject them all in favor of a different alternative. In this, we find encouragement from the Western scientific world-view, with its emphasis on single perspectives, verbal descriptions and "falsifiable hypotheses."

But superficially large differences may be only differences in viewpoint and in the choice of words, the results of limitations and fallibilities of human communication. Rather than con-centrating on differences, on "rejecting this because of that," we should try to apprehend the similarities in order to discern and understand the common underlying core.

You are more than just a material being of flesh and blood and matter. Your mind is more than simply electrical and chemical activity in your brain. You have nonmaterial aspects, too, without material limits and bounds. Your mind and all other minds are capable of filling and interpenetrating the universe and each other. This capability is independent of whether we characterize it in terms of higher selves, ki or ch'i flow, the Tao, the river of life or the hologram.

At the same time, your mind is also capable of perceiving itself as separate and distinct. The question of whether or not the mind is "really" separate from other minds is meaningless, like the question of whether the figure is "really" a B or a 13, or whether the water once in a glass still exists as distinct water once it has been dumped back in the river. These are not questions about reality in any absolute sense, but about perceptions of reality. They can be answered either way, depending on the perceptual elements you pull out of the rich reality "out there" and the way you assemble those elements into the more restricted personal reality you perceive at any particular moment.

If you have only experienced separateness, the idea that separateness results from your perception and is not an objective characteristic of the external world can be difficult to accept. I don't have a simple exercise to show you oneness, I'm afraid, though the following exercise may help. It should let you see the shift between a perception of separateness and oneness within your own body, and show you that your experience of yourself depends on which you choose. Similar shifts are possible, though more difficult to achieve, in your perception of your relationship with the rest of the world and in your resulting experience.

Go back to the first exercise in Chapter 1. Get your arms stuck with one arm pushing against the other. Notice how separate your arms are—separate from you as well as from each other. See how much conflict exists between them, and observe that it is the separateness which allows this conflict and prevents the arms from moving.

Without intentionally letting go of that conflict, realize that both arms are really integral parts of yourself, and perceive their unity with you. As you do, they will relax and the conflict will disappear. They will move anywhere you want them to, as a unit, but they will not fight one another. Then see them as separate again, and the conflict will reappear. Switch back and forth a few times—from separateness to oneness and back. Notice the switch between the two, like the switch between the B and the 13.

The same kind of switch exists for your perception of the relationship between you and the rest of the world. Just as in the exercise, you only experience conflict when you are switched to separateness. Conflict cannot exist when you are one with the world. Most of the time you choose separateness; your ego sees to that. But that is a choice *you* are making, albeit unconsciously, and not an objective characteristic of the way things are.

Earlier I likened consciousness to a light playing across the contents of the mind. You perceive separateness when that light is narrow, showing you things only a piece at a time. When you perceive a oneness with something or someone, that light is broader, illuminating you both in the same even light.

The contents of your mind are limitless. You can be aware of anything, if only you can bring consciousness to bear on it and hold it there. That is what I referred to earlier as "direct awareness." Apparently different psychic abilities such as telepathy or clairvoyance result from using that direct awareness differently, focusing it in different ways and on different things.

We are all psychic in the sense that we are capable of direct awareness of things outside our bodies. We make use of this direct awareness on a continuing basis, albeit subconsciously, in creating and maintaining our experiential reality. We have already seen the importance of the contraction reaction in creating the perception of solidity. When we contact something, we must contract and make ourselves rigid in order to perceive it as massive and solid. Yet this perception occurs even in the dark, with no sensory warning of impending contact. It can only be triggered by direct awareness that the object is there, operating below the level of consciousness.

The limits of our abilities to be conscious of our direct awareness are self-imposed limits on the way we *use* the mind, not absolute limits imposed by the nature of the mind. If absolute limits exist, they are so far beyond our self-imposed limits that for all practical purposes they are irrelevant. To say that our limits are self-imposed does not mean that they are not real limits. To say that all we need to do, in principle, is to refocus our consciousness does not mean that is easy to do in practice. The limits we place on ourselves are real, and they are highly effective for most people most of the time.

But those limits are not always completely effective. Everyone has flashes of direct awareness, but we usually paper them over and explain them away. These incidents take the form of "coincidences," like answering the phone to find someone on the line you were just thinking of calling, or "hunches" or "feelings" which turn out to be right. For some, they do take the form of full-fledged "psychic experiences," such as the sudden knowledge that a close relative has died, or a flash of precognitive awareness. Such experiences tend to be isolated events in this culture, but some cultures accept them as a normal part of everyday life. In *Primitive Psychic Power*, Ronald Rose describes instances of psychic awareness of death or illness in distant locations among Australian aborigines, and indicates that they considered such communication normal and routine.

Just as cultural variations exist in the use of direct awareness, so do individual variations. Some people have weaker internal barriers to direct awareness and are far more subject to psychic experience. These are the "natural psychics" in whom psychic abilities appear spontaneously, often in childhood.

Our barriers to direct awareness are not fixed and immutable from birth. To a large extent they are learned, and they can be unlearned. Thus psychic abilities can be cultivated, in the sense that the limits can be stretched, the barriers broken down. This can be done to some degree by deliberate effort—for example, by working on becoming more telepathic using exercises and feedback. One parapsychologist has even developed an ESP "teaching machine" for this purpose. Increases in psychic ability may also occur as by-products of more generalized personal growth, as the individual becomes more open and aware and "clears" the barriers which block awareness.

This second approach, generalized personal growth, has much to recommend it. Psychic ability, in and of itself, turns out to be far less useful than it might appear on the surface. Though it might seem otherwise, our primary limitations are not limitations on the information available to us, but on our abilities to understand and constructively use what is available.

A theme running through many Eastern teachings stresses that point. As you progress toward understanding and self-realization, according to this theme, you acquire supernatural powers as a matter of course. These should be ignored as much as possible, lest they distract you and become ends in themselves. Should this happen, they will "hang you up" and impede your further progress. Beyond that, the development of psychic powers per se is difficult because there is no such thing as "psychic powers" per se. There are no special "senses" of telepathy or clairvoyance which can be developed in and of themselves, the way you can develop large biceps or the ability to list all the state capitals. Rather, your psychic ability or lack thereof is an integral part of your total perceptual mechanism, of the way you construct your personal reality from the rich external reality.

We'll examine our barriers to direct awareness shortly, but first, here are two exercises to show you that awareness in ways you might not have noticed before. The first should let you see how subtle changes in your body reflect even minor changes in your surroundings—an instance of the Chinese idea that the microcosm within reflects the macrocosm without, perhaps. The second can be interpreted in the same way, or as a projection of part of your consciousness out of your body and into something else. As noted, these two explanations are not really different, but simply different sides of the same coin.

You may have heard of Rosa Kuleshova or other Russian psychics who can read with their fingertips. Our next exercise demonstrates a very rudimentary form of the same ability. You will need printed material containing two adjoining areas of different colors. Areas of solid color several inches wide are best. If you don't have anything else, the black "vase" in the illustration in the Introduction will do.

Close your eyes, and run your index finger back and forth from one area to the other. Relax, see how your finger feels, and notice any change as you move. After a few passes you should become aware of a subtle change as you cross the boundary between the colors. Slow down, and bring that change clearly to consciousness. Don't try to label it or talk to yourself about it, but just be aware of the sensation. When you have it clearly, stop your finger as the change occurs. Open your eyes and see how close to the boundary you are. With a little practice you should be able to stop at the boundary most of the time.

Don't actively *look* for the boundary. If you do, you're asking the ego to let you make a decision on the basis of information it doesn't think you should have. Just watch for the change in feeling, and let yourself find the boundary that way. Subtle changes in intention can make a lot of difference in what you experience.

You might wonder if you're just noticing subtle tactile differences in texture, with no "direct awareness" involved. If this concerns you, try the same exercise with a sheet of plastic or glass between your finger and the paper, or move your finger in the air slightly above the paper.

The next exercise will give you a chance to become aware of another living thing. The best subject to start with is a soaring bird, like a gull or a hawk. *Watch the bird with your eyes softly focused, i.e., have your attention on the bird, but without totally locking on to it. Relax. See the bird, and be aware of its movement. Empathize with it, and feel its movement with your body. Begin to notice your response to what the bird does.*

The transition between soaring and flapping flight is the easiest to catch. It's a little like the transition between the two different colors in the last exercise, except that you feel it in your whole body and not just your finger. Once you've caught the transition, you can go on to feel the different types of flight.

With practice, you can learn to feel other birds and animals as well. The main thing is to relax and tune yourself in to the movement, then feel changes in that movement. Watch for gross changes first—between soaring and flapping, resting and moving, and the like. The ability to feel more subtle changes will develop with experience.

There is a great gulf between noticing the boundary between two blocks of color and reading with your fingers, as some Russian psychics do. There is an equally great gulf between sensing the movements of a bird in flight and moving your consciousness about in space as Robert Monroe describes in *Journeys Out of the Body,* and as some yogis and shamans claim to do routinely. But in each case, the exercise shows you that the basic ability exists—to sense color with your finger or to focus your consciousness away from your body. Once you know that, the fact that people exist who have refined those abilities to high degrees should be no more unbelievable than the fact that there are acrobats whose balance and timing are far beyond the norm.

What kind of limitations do we place on ourselves? How do we erect these barriers that keep us so far from our potential, and why? Let's review some of these issues, then go on and explore them more deeply. The central fact to bear in mind is the immense richness of the reality "out there"—the over-abundance of information potentially available to us. There's too much to handle on a continuing basis, and it needs structure, anyway, if we are to make any sense of it. So we build models— internal representations of external reality—and we use those models to screen and filter our perceptions. We pick out and use cues the models say are relevant, and we block out and ignore the rest.

We could handle much more than we do on a continuing, conscious basis. The main reason for limiting ourselves is pure laziness. It's easier to minimize what we attend to consciously and to relegate as much as possible to "automatic" handling by our conditioned reflexes. When we do that long enough, we find it hard to reverse the process and take conscious control again. We even forget what we've lost, and we come to believe that our self-imposed limits represent the objective structure of the external world.

The part of the mind which handles the things we put on automatic is the ego. Acting as "chief of staff" to our conscious self, the ego controls the flow of information into consciousness and monitors and interprets the flow of orders back to the body. Like any good bureaucrat, the ego will try to do its job in what looks like the most efficient manner *from its point of view*. It will develop a simple view of reality, with clear sharp lines between the person and the rest of the world, and minimize the number of conflicts with that view which come into consciousness.

One way the ego does this is by keeping conscious attention within the physical body and brain. The external world is thus experienced through models constructed primarily from sensory inputs, with the role of direct awareness minimized. We model the world as a material place we can perceive only through our senses, then use that model to limit our awareness that we perceive it any other way.

Even when the body physically responds to information received through direct awareness, we may block that response from consciousness. Some of our earlier exercises have shown this, and it has been demonstrated in both American and Russian telepathy experiments. In one set of American experiments, the "receiver" was isolated in a soundproof room while his body signs (pulse, skin resistance, etc.) were measured on a polygraph. Elsewhere in the building the "sender" received electric shocks at random intervals. Asked to determine when these occurred, the receiver responded with random guesses; his conscious mind just didn't know. But his body did know, because his polygraph traces showed definite responses at the times the shocks were administered.

Comparable Russian experiments have yielded similar results. Changes in brain activity and body state (blood pressure, respiration, etc.) were induced telepathically and recorded by EEG's and other physiological monitoring equipment. If the receiver were sensitive enough, he would become conscious of these signals, but usually not until several seconds after his body began to respond. Some of these experiments were conducted over a distance of several hundred miles, indicating that distance is not a factor in the phenomenon.

We often don't notice low-level reactions like those picked up by the polygraphs in these experiments because we keep our mental environments fairly "noisy." We maintain high levels of ongoing internal activity—what don Juan calls the "internal dialogue" and Joseph Pearce calls "roof brain chatter." Part of this activity is verbal. The word machine runs on most of the time and we give our attention to the verbal thought stream instead of our direct experience. But much is also non-verbal. We constantly push, test and contract to keep the chair we sit in solid; we keep our visual images consistent with what we expect the world to contain; we otherwise maintain our experiential reality much as the ego wants it to be. One place I would quarrel with Pearce and Castaneda is that I believe they both give too much attention to the verbal part of the "internal dialogue" and not enough to the non-verbal part—the contraction reaction, level of body tension and the like.

You are your ego's greatest ally in the process of deceiving yourself. You let the ego control your consciousness so much of the time that the independent control you are capable of exercising becomes limited. You don't have enough control to focus your consciousness where *you* want it and hold it there, rather than letting the ego tell you where to put it. *Picture a door knob. Try to hold that picture in your mind for one minute, without other thoughts.* That should give you a chance to see some of the ego's distraction, the internal dialogue and your lack of control over your own consciousness. If you find it difficult to hold your consciousness focused on the simple image of a doorknob, no wonder you have trouble focusing it reliably on events outside your body.

Other problems you encounter in trying to focus consciousness on your direct awareness include knowing where to look, how to look, what to look for and how to interpret it once you find it. It's akin to the problem facing an illiterate aborigine in the Library of Congress. He's surrounded by information in forms he doesn't know how to use and exploit—in forms, in fact, that he may not even recognize as information.

The sensations and feeling I've pointed out to you through some of the exercises, such as the contraction reaction and the feeling of ch'i, are sensations and feelings you've had all your life. If you never saw them before, that's because you didn't know what to look for and didn't bother trying. To find them you need something to focus on, some way of directing your attention to where it needed to go and holding it there. I hope I've been successful in describing the exercises in a way that has provided that for you.

The real role, I believe, of much of the ritual and paraphernalia used by many psychics is to aid them in clearing their minds and focusing on the information they want to obtain. This is true even if the psychic believes the ritual has some magic power of its own, independent of the user. Just because someone can use her direct awareness does not mean that she understands how it works. Most psychics do not.

Extrasensory perception functions in the same way as the other perceptual processes we've looked at; selected cues combine with existing perceptual models to produce interpretative images of the things being perceived. The source of the cues may be different (direct awareness rather than some sensory mechanism) but the process remains subject to the same fallibilities and limitations. This is why so much psychically obtained information seems so vague, indefinite and ambiguous. Even the best psychics rely far more on their normal senses than on their psychic abilities. Their abilities to use and interpret psychic information simply haven't developed to the same degree as has, say, their vision. No wonder that direct awareness seems sporadic, unreliable and even non-existent in most of us.

We have well-developed forms of sensation and imagery associated with each of the senses—visual imagery with vision, sensations of touch and smell with those senses, etc. We have no corresponding imagery for direct awareness. We compensate by using sensory imagery as a way of presenting consciousness with information obtained through nonsensory means. The way someone perceives psychically obtained information thus depends on the kind of imagery her mind uses to present that information.

Some psychics see visions while others hear voices or feel tactile sensations, and others perceive some combination of these. Whatever the imagery, the images will be meaningful to the person involved, consistent with her experience and expectations. Christian mystics have visions of Christian saints but not of the Buddha, while for Buddhists the reverse obtains. Shamans have visions of sacred animals, demons, or whatever else their background teaches them to expect; and rational Westerners who have such experiences become paranoid schizophrenics, because it is "all in their heads."

The idea that the mind can use imagery associated with one of the senses to convey information from a different source may seem strange, but it occurs in contexts other than ESP as well. Dreaming involves the use of visual and auditory imagery to express feelings, emotions, needs and other internal thought-forms. In a sensory context, there are people who "see" sounds or other nonvisual stimuli, in the sense that those stimuli produce visual imagery for them. This condition is called synesthesia, and individuals who perceive in this way are called synesthetes.

Synesthetes may see abstract moving shapes and changing colors in response to words or music. A particular word may seem "blue," a piece of music "swirly." Like natural psychics, synesthetes often grow up thinking everyone else perceives the world as they do. The husband of one synesthete described her reaction when she found he was not synesthetic as one of pity. What a drab world he must live in, she thought, where sounds had no colors and words had no shape.

When the mind uses visual imagery to depict scenes sensed through direct awareness, we should not expect those scenes to appear exactly as they would to the eyes. Different perceptual cues are being filtered through different perceptual models, and different processes are involved in translating the images into visual form.

To understand this better, think again of your vision as a process in which an artist within you looks at a scene, picks out the elements she thinks are important, and sketches those elements. Your visual image of the scene, then, is her finished sketch. When the scene is "viewed" with direct awareness, the artist can't see it in the same way. Rather, it is as if someone else were viewing the scene and describing it to the artist, who was then trying to sketch it on the basis of that verbal description. No wonder that the two images differ.

This is why places, people and even visual patterns look different in "visions" than they do when viewed with the eyes. In *Journeys Out of the Body,* for example, Robert Monroe describes out-of-body experiences in which he "viewed" people he knew but didn't recognize them for who they were. When I first read the book, I found those accounts troubling. If he had really "seen" his acquaintances, I thought, why hadn't he recognized them? As I came to understand the nature of perception, the answer became clear. A visual image constructed from direct awareness is just not the same as a visual image constructed from visual information provided by the eyes.

THE NATURE OF MAGIC

The mind not only knows the world but affects it as well, in non-ordinary ways. I will refer to such phenomena as *magic* and to the people responsible for them as *magicians*.

The first specific forms of magic I want to consider are the internal martial arts such as T'ai Chi and Aikido, as performed by true masters of those arts. If you have not experienced these arts at the hands of a master, you may think it strange to call them "magic." But they are magic, properly done, in the sense that the practitioner perceives the world in a non-ordinary way, and through that perception manipulates the world (in particular, his opponent) in a manner not ordinarily possible. The qualifier *properly done* is an important one here, in that few practitioners of these arts really do them properly. Most do them as largely external arts (like judo, karate and the hard styles of kung fu), depending on little more than the skillful manipulation of strength, speed and balance within the framework of ordinary reality.

Physical interactions take place as they normally do because all parties participate in the ordinary-reality consensus about such interactions. A T'ai Chi master in combat does not participate in that consensus. As a result, he cannot be grabbed, held, punched or otherwise attacked, and he can toss his opponent away with a flick of the wrist. Being on the receiving end of this kind of skill evokes feelings of confusion and helplessness. You grab and there's nothing to hold on to; you swing and miss, even though he doesn't seem to have moved. He moves, and suddenly you are falling or flying helplessly through the air.

The T'ai Chi master is not actively "doing" anything to bring this about. Rather, he is "not-doing" in the sense that don Juan uses that term. He is not responding to the actions of his opponent as his opponent unconsciously expects and needs him to. The opponent cannot deal with that non-response and defeats himself with his own reactions to it. The T'ai Chi master Yang Chen-Fu likened "correct technique" to leading a thousand pound cow by a string through its nose. The cow is too heavy to move with force, but the string induces it to move in the direction the person holding the string wants it to go.

Remember the wrist-grasping exercise in Chapter 5 which showed you the contraction response. *Go back to that exercise and try it again. This time,* you tell yourself *"that's holding"* as *your friend grasps* and *"that's releasing"* as she releases your *wrist. When you have the reaction clearly in focus, try to stay relaxed, tell yourself "that's releasing," and inhibit the contraction of your wrist* as your friend grabs. *You probably won't stop the grab altogether (though you might) but it should be considerably weaker and looser than it is when you contract.*

Your contraction is an integral part of your agreement to the consensus reality within which the grasping occurs. Similar contractions are necessary for you to be restrained (e.g., the exercise in the chair in Chapter 5 or the exercise holding your own wrist earlier in this chapter) or even struck. Someone attempting to grasp, hold or strike you depends on those responses; he cannot carry out his intention unless he obtains them. The T'ai Chi master does not provide them.

The T'ai Chi master tosses his opponent away in the same manner. He moves his hand, but without the contraction that normal physical contact would require. The opponent must choose (again, subconsciously) between allowing contact without contraction or keeping out of the way of the contact altogether. The former represents more of a break with consensus reality than he can tolerate, so he chooses the latter. He levitates out of the way and interprets the experience as having been effortlessly tossed aside by the T'ai Chi master. (I'll have more to say about levitation shortly.)

Plato compared our perceptions of reality to shadows on the wall of a cave. Earlier I suggested that what we perceive as ordinary physical interactions are actually the result of elaborate rules of conduct governing the behavior of those shadows. In terms of this metaphor, the T'ai Chi master doesn't play by the rules. When his shadow comes in contact with his opponent's shadow, he does not observe the consensual ritual of contraction and pushing to determine which shadow should give way to the other; he keeps right on moving. The opponent must then move his shadow out of the way or allow the shadows to overlap. The latter is unthinkable, so he does the former.

Once we understand T'ai Chi, it's easier to understand other forms of magic involving the reactions of living things—forms such as hunting-magic, healing-magic and the casting of spells.

We need only remember that the connections between living things are not all material ones. Everything is connected to everything else at nonmaterial levels. If the magician can focus and bring to awareness the connections between him and his subject, he can alter those connections. The subject will respond to those alterations. To the extent that the magician can produce a predictable response, he can influence the behavior of the subject.

This is by no means easy. It requires exceptional mental control and for this reason is extremely rare. But it does happen. The fetishes, dolls, drawings and other paraphernalia often employed to do magic only aid the magician in directing and focusing the mind. They have no magical power per se, even if the magician believes that they do. Rather, it is the ability to disturb the subject's existing balance which allows the magician to influence the subject, and the subject's response to that disturbance which actually produces the effect.

In healing, for example, the healer induces the patient to break down the barriers he has erected between himself and his illness, and take positive control of his own body again. The healer may also provide the patient with some supplemental energy to aid in the process (as in the exercise in Chapter 8). The particular explanatory model the healer evokes will, of course, depend on his culture and belief system.

Some argue that magic can have an effect only if the subject believes in it, because only then will he respond to the knowledge that he is under a spell. That argument is half right; it correctly identifies the subject's response as the source of the magical effect. It is wrong, however, about the way that response is activated. The term "belief" usually refers to someone's conscious, intellectual understanding of the world, and that is not what matters. Rather, it is the subject's involuntary (usually subconscious) *response patterns*, and how those patterns lead him to respond to the magician's disturbance. Fire can burn you because of the way you respond to it, not because you believe in it, and magic works in the same way.

That brings us to the next category of magic—firewalking, "superhuman" feats of strength and levitation, etc. The subject of the magic in this case is the magician who acts in ways which seem to violate some "law of nature." The explanation lies in the fact that the mechanism which normally brings about the outcome we expect (the one the magician avoids) is not a law of nature at all, but an involuntary conditioned response. The magician has overcome this conditioning and need not respond in that manner. Thus he has the ability to produce a different outcome. It is the same basic mechanism we've seen in the case of T'ai Chi, now applied to interactions with inanimate objects.

Let's begin with a fairly mundane phenomenon—electric shock—and look at the mechanism involved. The severity of the shock you receive when you touch a live electrical wire depends on the amount of electrical current passing through your body. This depends in turn on the voltage of the source and on the electrical resistance through your body to ground. For any given voltage, less current will flow (and you will experience less shock) if the resistance is high than if it is low. That is why the shock will be worse if you're standing in water than if you're on a dry surface wearing leather soled shoes.

Your body itself provides a major source of electrical resistance. If your body's resistance is high, you will receive less of a shock than if it is low. But this is a function of the level of tension in your body—in other words, of the degree to which you are contracted. When you are calm and relaxed, your resistance is high; when you become nervous or tense, it drops. The galvanic skin response channel on a polygraph takes advantage of this, and of the fact that when you tell a lie you involuntarily contract. The abrupt decrease in resistance shows up as a sudden change in the GSR measurement.

This means that (all other factors being equal) you will receive less of a shock if you are calm and relaxed than you will if you are nervous and tense. (And if you are relaxed enough, you will hardly feel a shock at all.) But the normal conditioned response to electric shock is to contract and tense your body. This causes your body's electrical resistance to drop and increases the severity of the shock. In this situation, as in many others, the external threat can harm you only because you react in a way that allows that harm to occur.

The same thing happens when you contact something hot. You contract, and that contraction enhances the transfer of heat into the body. If the source of heat is intense enough, you get burned, perhaps seriously. Yet there are exceptions. Traditional cultures all over the world—in Europe, Asia and in the Americas—have religious rituals in which people routinely walk across white-hot coals without getting burned. In an altered state of consciousness the firewalkers perceive the world in a way which allows them to remain relaxed and calm, and the fire does not burn.

Being burned, like being grabbed, getting sick or getting a shock from a live wire, is an interaction with the world that requires your acquiescence and participation, albeit unconscious and involuntary. You participate by contracting and withdrawing from the point of contact between you and the fire. This withdrawal is what allows the transfer of heat which causes the burn. Without it, enough heat would not be transferred to burn you. The firewalkers inhibit this withdrawal, and they don't get burned.

Let me emphasize the point made earlier about belief. No matter how much you *believe* that you can walk across hot coals, if you contract and withdraw awareness as you step out on the coals your feet will be badly burned. Conversely, even if you don't believe it is possible, if you step out on the coals without contracting you will be able to walk across them without harm. There are reports of skeptical Western observers at firewalking ceremonies being led across the coals by the priests conducting the ceremony. Apparently these priests were able to show the observers (with touch, in a non-intellectual way) how to walk on the coals without contracting, in spite of their intellectual disbelief in the possibility.

We have already talked about feats of superhuman strength, such as the kid who lifted the car off his father when it fell off the jack. Most of the effort we put into any muscular activity is wasted energy. It goes into tensing muscles against each other to provide the sensation of working against external resistance. The amount of energy actually required by the task itself is always small, even negligible. Anyone who directs himself to the task alone, then, without using energy to uselessly push against himself, will appear to possess superhuman strength. He will be able to move heavy objects, or hold a heavy bow at full draw with relaxed arms.

Let's look now at levitation. Gravity, like electric shock, fire or physical contact, is a force we are subject to because we choose to be. Gravity acts on us, in other words, because we perceive that to be the case. We look for and try to maintain a firm foundation under us, and we "fall" when we can't find one. Like going rigid in response to solidity and being burned in response to fire, the maintenance of that foundation can be at least partially inhibited in some circumstances. Castaneda characterizes don Juan as "incredibly agile" for a man of his age, describing situations in which he seems to be on his feet instantly, without getting up in the usual sense. Jesus is said to have walked on water; and critics sometimes describe exceptional ballet dancers, with more truth than they know, as "gravity defying."

We can all levitate. In fact, we do it all the time. But like direct awareness, we suppress conscious awareness of it. Levitation is the direction of movement by the mind, and all movement involves levitation. You levitate when you raise your arm, walk or get out of a chair. The muscular force you expend in the process is incidental, like the force you expend making yourself rigid when you encounter a "solid" object. It serves to maintain your *perception* of your experiential reality, but is not an *essential* part of your interaction with the external world. Even falling is levitating downward, looking for a place to find support.

Reach up and touch your hair, and see how effortlessly your arm responds to your intention. Notice that the upward impetus occurs in the arm and wrist—not back in the shoulder muscles which the Western model sees as the source of the movement. Raise your arm first by thinking about moving the hand, then the wrist, and finally the forearm; see if you can notice the difference. The same gross physical motion occurs in each case, but the feeling which produces the motion is different.

You become stuck by inhibiting your levitation. In effect, you forget how to levitate. Putting more effort into trying to move (without levitating) won't help; it just makes you more rigid and increases the feeling of stuckness. The following exercise is intended to show you this. It is difficult, in the sense that the changes you have to look for are more subtle than in most of the previous exercises. But with close attention you should be able to find them and perhaps gain a major insight into the nature of movement.

Sit so that you can comfortably rest your right arm on a table. Raise your arm several inches into the air, then let it sink back and rest on the table again. Repeat this movement many times, gradually allowing yourself to see the movement with greater detail and clarity. Notice that as your arm comes to rest on the table, you experience a feeling of settling and emptying, as though something were leaving your arm and flowing into the table. As you prepare to raise your arm, and as it begins to come up, notice the reverse feeling of filling and putting back. Continue raising and lowering your arm until you see these transitions clearly. It's as though your arm gives something to the table in order to rest there and takes it back in order to move again.

Once you've come to see that, don't put it back. Let your arm empty as it comes to rest on the table, then consciously inhibit the feeling of "putting back." With that feeling inhibited, try to raise your arm with muscular effort alone. The feeling of "putting back" is the feeling of preparing your arm to levitate. If you can successfully inhibit that feeling, you won't be able to lift your arm.

When you've done that, try the following variation. Let your arm come to rest on the table, and feel it empty. Have a friend hold your arm down, and try to pick it up. Notice that you can't seem to figure out how to fill your arm again with your friend holding it, and that's the reason you can't pick it up. That's what I meant by saying that we get stuck by "forgetting" how to levitate.

Go back and review the earlier exercises involving "getting stuck," beginning with the arm-holding exercise in Chapter 1, in the light of what you've just done. You should be able to see all of them now from this perspective. You respond to the perception of a barrier by inhibiting your ability to levitate— your ability to move. You then put muscular energy into tensing muscles and becoming rigid, but that doesn't help you move because it has nothing to do with moving. You can't really see the kind of choice you make in being stuck in response to an external constraint until you can learn to make yourself stuck in the absence of any such constraint. That is the value to an exercise like this.

All this boils down to the idea I started with. The reality you experience is not an "objective" material world "out there." It is your own construction, your way of choosing from and interacting with a reality far richer in potential than you can ever imagine. The limits you experience are not external limits imposed by the nature of that outside reality, but internal limits you impose on yourself. The agreement you find with others about what the world is like results from the fact that we all learn to construct our individual realities in much the same way. That agreement thus causes the appearance of an objective external reality, rather than resulting from the existence of one.

We are all psychics and magicians, possessing direct awareness of the world around us and the ability to levitate our physical bodies. We use these abilities continuously in creating and maintaining our individual experiential realities, but we suppress conscious awareness of them. Many things we regard as paranormal abilities, such as superhuman strength or firewalking, are not really abilities at all; they are just different choices in creating and interacting with the world.

We usually think of perceiving and interacting with the world as quite different processes. We see perceiving as passive, a simple process of sensing and being aware of things which exist independent of our awareness of them. Interaction we see as more active, involving doing things to the world and having an effect on it. But that distinction is artificial, created by the illusion of an objective external reality. Perception and interaction are inexorably intertwined and cannot be separated. How can we passively perceive "solidity," for example, when that perception is a product of the way we choose to interact?

10
Learning and Growing

Some of the ideas discussed here have unsettling implications. Not the least of these is that we have a great deal more potential for control over our lives, individually and collectively, than we normally think possible. If that is the case, why do we do such a lousy job of it? Why do we create a world so full of misery, unhappiness and trouble? Why do these things seem so difficult to change? What's the purpose of it all, anyway?

These sorts of questions fall within the realm thought of as "religious," and before dealing with them we need to look briefly at the subject of religion. There are important parallels with science (Chapter 6), though the diversity of belief systems and ways of articulating those systems make religion a much more complex subject. An analysis of religion to even the shallow depth to which I examined science would take a book in itself, so I will only sketch the broad conclusions which I believe such an analysis would reach.

The term *religion* encompasses a wide range of human institutions and belief systems, with as many significant differences among them as similarities. For this reason, it seems appropriate to use the plural *religions* rather than the singular to refer to this collection of institutions. Religions, like science, are attempts to understand the world and our place in it. They focus on somewhat different questions than does science, though important overlaps do exist. Both are ultimately concerned with the nature of the world and how it works in a fundamental sense. Religions seek their answers in different ways from science, though the underlying processes have commonalities. Both can be thought of as collective perceptual processes in which selected cues from "out there" are combined with previously held models to construct images of reality then thought of as knowledge.

An area of major difference between science and religion—and indeed, of wide variability among religions—concerns the way knowledge is codified in verbal form. Science uses language quite literally, intending scientific knowledge to be accurately and completely codified in the words used to represent it. A few religions, such as fundamentalist sects, interpret their teachings in a similar literal fashion. Most religions, however, acknowledge some degree of symbolism. The meaning of their teachings can thus only be understood by going beyond the words to the underlying concepts. A few, such as some forms of Buddhism, claim that the verbal dogma is meaningless by itself and that the essence of their teachings can be understood only through direct experience.

This makes the interpretation of religious teachings a difficult task, particularly for outsiders with a different background of experience. Even members of the religion living in a different time, place and culture may misinterpret their own teachings. Many fundamentalists choose to interpret the Bible literally, for example, though it is far from clear that its writers intended it to be taken that way.

Religions are more than collective perceptual processes; they are also social and political institutions (as is science). As such, they are concerned with mundane issues such as institutional survival, expansion and political power, and these concerns affect their formulation and interpretation of dogma. Many religions choose to establish themselves as mediators between their adherents and whatever gods or higher powers they recognize. In this way they create and maintain a continuing need for the institution in the lives of its members.

Consider Christianity, for example. Jesus preached the immediacy of the "kingdom of heaven." He said that all men could do as he did—could create the same kinds of miracles— if they accepted that kingdom. He preached, in other words, a doctrine that each person was responsible for his or her own reality. Such a doctrine could hardly sustain a large bureaucracy for two thousand years, however. Thus orthodox Christian dogma has put far more emphasis on the role of the church as intervener between man and God.

I view religious teachings in the same way I view scientific knowledge and the models of health and healing used by various healing traditions—as partial, incomplete and sometimes distorted representations of a common underlying reality. What follows will focus on what I see as some of the core ideas in that underlying reality, occasionally pointing out where I believe particular teachings distort the ideas they represent. As in the rest of the book I will try to be descriptive rather than prescriptive—to deal with things as they are, not to tell you what to do about them. That choice, as always, is yours.

At one level I have already answered the question of why we create the kind of world we do. We create it because it's the one we learned how to create from our culture, the one produced by our conditioned responses. But that answer isn't really satisfactory, because it leaves open the questions of why we have those choices in the first place, and of the purpose behind the whole thing.

To attempt to answer those questions, it is necessary to speculate about the nature of the larger system of which we are part and our role in that system. I want to emphasize the word *speculate* here, because that is really all we can do. We can look at various possibilities and see what seems the most reasonable, but there's no objective way of deciding. In the final analysis, the scientist's belief that the world is a material system in which life evolved by chance is just as unprovable as the fundamentalist's belief that God created the world and everything in it in 4004 B.C. Granting that, my speculation on those questions follows.

The Western world-view, as already noted, sees the physical

material world as the primary ground of existence, with life and consciousness as accidental byproducts of electrical and chemical activity within that physical, material world. I have argued that that is not the case, that mind has an existence of its own independent of the material world. I now want to take that argument a step further. I believe a relationship does exist between mind and the physical world, but in the other direction. The material world (or at least the appearance of a material world) is a by-product of mind—of our individual minds and of the collective mind, whatever that is.

The fundamental stuff of the world is *mindstuff*. The material world is an illusion, a creation of mindstuff within which to explore the nature of physical experience. We are part of that mindstuff and part of that exploration. Our fundamental purposes as intelligent beings are *learning* and *growth*, and the apparent reality we create and inhabit is a training aid to help us achieve those purposes. It provides an environment in which we can experience and learn to understand the consequences of our actions and decisions.

Our world is the way it is because of the choices we have made, individually and collectively. We have chosen, for example, to ignore the long-range effects of many of our actions, producing the environmental destruction and pollution we see around us. We have chosen to reduce our death rate without making corresponding changes in our birthrate, and over-population is the result. We have chosen to focus on the external world and neglect the internal and have created a highly mechanistic technological society. Individually, we choose to accept the world defined for us by our culture, and we reap the consequences of living in that world.

Think again about the analogy between life and a board game like *Monopoly*. The world is the game board, and we are the pieces. We move about the board constrained by rules which specify what moves we can make and what we can know to make them. But unlike *Monopoly*, the rules aren't imposed from the outside. We make them ourselves—individually and through the collective process called culture. And we each have the right and the ability to change them—at least so far as they apply to us personally—if we are willing to go to the trouble to do so.

That's what the game is ultimately about—learning how it works and how to relax the artificial constraints you place on yourself. Once you see that, really see that, you are no longer caught by the game, even though you continue to play. That's what Eastern religions call "enlightenment" and what don Juan calls "controlled folly," in contrast to the plain "folly" the rest of us engage in.

I am not using the term *game* to suggest anything frivolous or purely entertaining. Rather, it should suggest that life can be viewed from a broader perspective and seen as something we do within a constrained context with a specified playing area, rules limiting the moves we can make, etc. In *The Ultimate Athlete*, George Leonard develops this characterization of the game in greater depth. The "ultimate athlete" in his title of that book is the player in that game, each one of us.

The game of life provides each of us with a continuing flow of experience to interpret and interact with. We filter that flow through our perceptual models, selecting out cues which we interpret through those models and sometimes use to modify the models themselves. It is only in this last instance—when we allow the new information to modify our existing models rather than just using the models to interpret the information—that learning occurs. In the "red spade" experiment described earlier, for example, learning occurred only when the subjects realized they were seeing anomalous cards and modified their perceptual models accordingly.

There are different types of learning and they occur on different levels. The simplest type consists of *accumulating details*. Memorizing the capitals of the states, or learning a new recipe once you already know how to cook, would be examples of this type of learning. It's just a matter of adding new facts or details, with no new concepts or changes in existing concepts. Much formal education consists of this type of learning, as does most "normal science."

Sometimes the material accumulated takes us beyond the limits of our existing perceptual models. Learning then requires the *creation of new models*, of a new framework into which the material can be placed. We do a lot of this as infants—learning to see, to hear, to feel texture and solidity. We do more of it as we grow, learning new concepts and using those concepts to structure our understanding of the world. This kind of learning is important in education—for example, in learning to read or to do arithmetic. It also plays a role in "normal science," or in any endeavor where we significantly *expand* the boundaries of the "known" to include things which were previously "unknown."

But not all learning expands the boundaries of the known, in the sense of simply moving those boundaries out to encompass more. Some learning contracts those boundaries as well, as new understanding invalidates previous "knowledge." Seeing a red spade for the first time doesn't just add a new category to your existing perceptual model of playing cards. It contradicts that model, implying that something you previously "knew" to be true is really false.

When existing understanding and new experience conflict, one must be denied. Often we deny the new experience. We see the red spade as a heart, and we fail to notice the experiential anomalies which would contradict our current world-view. Many who consider themselves "scientifically minded" refuse to acknowledge the large body of evidence for the existence of paranormal phenomena, secure in a world model which "proves" such phenomena to be impossible. Normal science can continue for a long time in the presence of major anomalies; yet once a revolution occurs, those anomalies appear so obvious that it seems amazing that they could have been tolerated so long.

If we deny the new experience, learning cannot take place. When it does, the learning takes the form of a *model revision*, replacing an existing perceptual model with one better suited to the world now perceived. Seeing a red spade for the first time is one example of this kind of learning, as is seeing a 13 instead of a B. Other examples might include a scientific revolution such as the "discovery" of oxygen, in which the existing scientific paradigm (phlogiston, in that case) is replaced by a new one, or a religious conversion in which a new faith becomes dominant in someone's life. Even the gradual process of alienation and estrangement leading to dissolution of a once-happy marriage can be seen as a process of model revision.

These examples each involve replacing an existing model with one on much the same level, in the sense that the new model describes a more or less equivalent part of the world from a new perspective. In yet another form of learning, which might be called a *level shift*, the old model is not simply replaced by a new one. Rather, a new *way* of seeing the world is found, a shift to a different level of understanding.

Seeing a 13 instead of a B is a model revision, as is seeing oxygen instead of phlogiston or substituting one set of gods for another. To see that the B/13 is really neither, but a perceptual choice, produces a level shift. To see, as Thomas Kuhn did, that phlogiston and oxygen are *both* intellectual constructs used to explain different but overlapping sets of facts takes a level shift, as does seeing that two different sets of gods are different ways of symbolizing man's relationship with a larger universe. Seeing a red spade for the first time involves a model revision, and that lets you see more red spades in the future. But understanding the implications of that red spade for the nature of perception produces a level shift.

We can illustrate each of these types of learning in the metaphor of painting a picture of a three-dimensional scene. Accumulating detail is just that—adding more detail to elements of the scene already sketched in. Creating a new model is analogous to extending the picture to parts of the scene not previously included. Model revision corresponds to moving to a new perspective and modifying the picture accordingly, as we saw when we looked at scientific revolution. A level shift is qualitatively different, involving a shift of focus from the picture to the scene itself and the realization that the picture is only a partial and incomplete representation of the scene, no matter what perspective is chosen and how much detail included.

Sharply defined boundaries do not exist between these different types of learning. One shades into another, depending on how you choose to identify the elements involved in particular instances. What looks like a model revision to you might look like a level shift to me, and like the creation of a new model to somebody else. Nonetheless, these different types of learning do exemplify important qualitative differences in the

kinds of learning we undergo. Our ability to experience each
when appropriate determines our capability for growth.

I identified *growth* as our second purpose, in addition to
learning, as intelligent beings. I see growth as continued movement toward a broader and fuller understanding of the nature of
things—toward knowing that life is a game and understanding
what that game is about. Growth involves learning, but it is
more. You can spend years learning more and more without
growing at all, and in many ways Western society encourages
this.

Growth is a process of movement to which learning contributes. All forms of learning are necessary, each in its time
and place. At times growth requires the accumulation of detail
and nothing more. This may be the case when you have just
passed through a learning experience of one of the other types
and need to consolidate and fill out the insights. This may also
be the case when you first begin to venture into a new area and
don't yet know enough to begin to form a coherent picture.

At other times you may be overloaded with details. You need
no more additional data, but a new conceptual lens through
which to view the data. The lens might take the form of a new
perceptual model not inconsistent with those you already hold,
or it may require some revision of existing models. Sometimes
this can be done at the same level, and at other times a level
shift is needed. Any of these processes may take place so
gradually you hardly notice or may happen so suddenly that
you are left shaken and breathless.

Growth is a natural process, like water running downhill. It
may even be an inevitable one. You can impede its progress,
slow it down, and even stop it for periods of time, but the
pressures for growth will remain. Eventually, those pressures
increase beyond containment, breaking down whatever im-
pediments exist and allowing growth to continue its slow but
inexorable course.

Impede it we do! Individually and collectively, we create
major barriers to our own and others' growth. Before discussing
some of these barriers, I want to look at the question of time
scale—of how long the game goes on and how many times we
play it. From a corporeal perspective, that translates into the

question of life after death. Of the many views on that question held by various human societies, I now find the concept of reincarnation—the idea that the same "self" lives many life-times—the most reasonable. I will briefly describe how my views on that subject evolved and how they fit in with the ideas this book is about.

I was raised as a Methodist and taught that good people go to Heaven when they die while bad people go to Hell. Even as a kid, I found those teachings hard to accept, and by the time I was in college, I had totally rejected them. Life, I had come to believe, was a by-product of electrical and chemical activity in the body and stopped when that activity ceased. I saw no reason to assume any continuity of consciousness beyond death and felt that to do so was fantasy and wishful thinking.

What little I knew about different views of life after death seemed to support that conclusion, since those views appeared so different and incompatible that they couldn't be describing the same objective conditions. Having reached that conclusion, I set it aside and ignored it. I "knew" that life ended with death, just as I knew, say, that most of the earth's surface was water. Neither fact, however, required much conscious thought in my day-to-day life.

As my world-view began to broaden in the directions which led to this book, I was not particularly concerned with the question of life after death. It arose more or less spontaneously, as part of the natural flow of the conceptual change I was experiencing. It arose first, in fact, as the question of "life during life"—the question of what "I" as a human being was really like. As I came to see that there was more "out there" then just the apparent material world, I began to consider the possibility that "I" was more than just what lived in my body. I eventually concluded this was so, in a sense I don't fully understand but can symbolize through the metaphor of the *Monopoly* marker in the game of life and the larger player sitting outside the game looking in.

Once I came to see things that way, the belief that life ended with death was no longer tenable. That belief had been based on a physical/material model of reality. With that model rejected, the basis for the belief was gone. Once I conceived

of myself as part of a larger entity, it made no sense to assume
that the larger entity "died" when it stopped using my body.

Think of yourself as a *Monopoly* marker, conscious of the
board and the game while it is being played, and "dying" when
the game is over. If you identify with the piece and see no world
beyond the game, then the conclusion that "life" ends with
"death" seems reasonable. Now see yourself instead as an
extension of (or perhaps, as Seth says, a fragment of) the player.
From that perspective, to conclude that life ends with death is
equivalent to concluding that the player dies when he puts
away the game.

I found further evidence that consciousness may transcend
death in the work of Dr. Elizabeth Kubler-Ross, author of
Death, the Final Stage of Growth and other books about death,
and Dr. Raymond Moody, author of *Life after Life*. Independently, these two physicians had talked to hundreds of
people who had been near death and survived. Many of those
they interviewed had been conscious during the experience,
and their experiences had been remarkably similar.

These experiences, moreover, closely paralleled the first
stages of the after-death experience as described in such
sources as the *Tibetan Book of the Dead* and the *Egyptian Book
of the Dead*, traditional teachings intended to assist in the
life-to-death transition. Similar descriptions of the death
experience can be found in other cultures, including medieval
European writings, and even in discussions of out-of-body
phenomena, such as Robert Monroe's *Journeys Out of the Body*.

The common elements which run through these varied
accounts include a separation of consciousness from the body,
accompanied by a feeling of well-being and an end to bodily
discomfort and pain. Usually the person remains in the
immediate vicinity of the body for a while, aware of the
corporeal events taking place around him—attempts to revive
him and the like—and in near-death experiences, he often
reenters the body at that point.

He may be met by "greeters" who seem to be there to aid the
transition. These may be friends and relatives who died earlier
or religious figures who are meaningful to him. For some, they
are simply disincarnate "presences."

The dying person usually has a chance to review his life and see what it has taught him—a kind of "after game debriefing," perhaps. The "life passing before my eyes" commonly associated with near-death experiences such as almost drowning is probably a version of this review, as is the "judgment before St. Peter" of Christian tradition. After death the person passes to the appropriate afterworld, according to some traditions, perhaps eventually to reincarnate again in human form.

Noticeable differences exist in the details of the descriptions provided by different people and cultures. Buddhists encounter demons, both good and bad, while Christians encounter saints and angels. The review is simply a review for some and a formal celestial court for others. In some traditions the deceased goes on to a non-earthly afterlife, while in others he eventually reincarnates. Superficially, these differences appear great enough to preclude the possibility that the descriptions all refer to the same events. Some people use this (as I once did) to argue that the descriptions must therefore be myth and superstition, with no real basis in fact.

But perception, as we have seen, is a more subjective phenomenon than we ordinarily realize. The high degree of agreement we usually find results from our consensus on how to perceive the world, not from its objective characteristics. The death experience, like "psychic" awareness, lies outside the bounds of our usual consensus. We should expect that experience to vary widely and different individuals to perceive it in terms consistent with their background and expectations. The more sophisticated treatments of the subject, such as the *Tibetan Book of the Dead*, clearly state that the demons and apparitions experienced by the deceased are constructs of his individual psyche without objective reality.

In the light of all this, the argument that life ends with death appears untenable. It seems far more likely that consciousness continues beyond death, perhaps through a series of lives and deaths. For a number of reasons, I find this possibility more likely than a single earthly life followed by an eternal "here-after." Belief in some form of reincarnation is widely held among human cultures, including cultures which show far more sophistication about such things than does ours. Belief in an eternal afterlife without reincarnation may result from an incomplete understanding of the process—an awareness that does not go beyond the early stages of life after death, like my two-year-old son's belief that I spent my entire business trip in the airplane. In terms of the game metaphor, if life is a training aid, it seems reasonable that most players could get more out of it by playing it more than once, particularly in view of how little many people seem to learn in one pass through.

That brings us back to the questions of learning and growth. If we take the possibility of reincarnation at all seriously—not necessarily "believe in" it, but just consider it a serious possibility—then we must look at learning and growth on a time scale longer than a single lifetime. Only from such a perspective, in fact, does it make sense to characterize growth as inevitable; it is clearly not inevitable in a single lifetime. If we do live many lifetimes, play the game many times, then it seems likely that those "plays" are related. Our growth or lack thereof in one lifetime will affect what we do in the next. I don't believe that specific events in one life are directly connected to specific events in another—that, for example, a particular transgression now will result in specific punishment the next time around. That view, I think, represents an over-simplified perception of a larger but vaguer truth—the *Monopoly* marker's attempt to explain the player's broad patterns of play in terms of the limited reality of the *Monopoly* board.

It seems more plausible that the basic patterns of perception and interaction we learn in one lifetime carry over to and provide the starting point for the next. During that life, our learning and experience modify them, and we carry the modified patterns on to the next. Eventually, as we come to understand what the game has to teach, we no longer need to play it. We can then go on to whatever comes next, which may be as far beyond our human comprehension as our human world is beyond the comprehension of the *Monopoly* marker.

Specific conflicts or other situations do not carry over directly. To the extent that they result from our conditioned patterns of perception and interaction, however, the effect is much the same. I may live in a hostile and lonely world, for example, because I perceive it as such and interact with it in a manner that keeps it that way. If I do nothing to change those interaction patterns, I will carry them with me into my next life and find that world a hostile and lonely place as well. I can escape from it only when I learn that the hostility comes from me and the outside world simply reflects it back.

Some of these issues were brought into sharper focus for me several years ago when a friend unsuccessfully attempted suicide. He was a capable scientist just embarking on what promised to be a highly successful career. His professional future seemed assured, and by all the usual external indicators of success, he had it made. At the same time, he was a victim of the psychological fragmentation so prevalent in contemporary society. He had serious problems with his personal life, centering around difficulties in maintaining emotional relationships. He saw his future as more of the same—professional success accompanied by personal loneliness and feelings of inadequacy. Oblivion seemed preferable, so he tried to kill himself and failed.

I have always believed that an individual's right to control his own life includes the right to end it if he finds it intolerable. At the time my friend made his attempt, though, I had not given any recent thought to the consequences of that act, or to how my own changes in world-view had affected my perception of them. The discussions we had as he was recovering gave me a good chance to think about those issues, and forced him to think about them as well.

My friend chose suicide in the belief that it would bring total oblivion—"like going to sleep and not waking up." Neither he nor his problems would exist any more. Once I would have thought the same thing, but I was now unsure. Suppose, I suggested, that it didn't work out that way, and that instead of oblivion he found another life with much the same set of problems, though perhaps in an altered form. What if there weren't any escape, but only the chance to keep doing it (life) over again until he got it right. This was a serious suicide attempt, not a device to get attention. When he found out he had failed, some of his first thoughts concerned how to be sure his next attempt succeeded. He hasn't made another attempt, and he's now seriously trying to understand and deal with his problems. That's due in part, I think, to the doubts I raised about what the consequences of "success" might be.

Growth can be a painful process, and we all try to avoid pain. Often it cannot be avoided but only delayed. The longer we delay, the more it may eventually hurt, for our attempt to avoid it can be the real source of the pain. Suicide is not a good way to avoid pain; it does nothing about the basic patterns causing the problem. You carry those same patterns along for next time, but you give up whatever insights you might have accumulated into what they are and how to change them.

Growth involves continuing movement toward a broader and fuller understanding of ourselves and our place in the world. Within a single lifetime, growth begins in infancy and continues throughout life. At least, that should happen, if the individual and her culture allow it to happen that way. But we establish barriers to growth and put obstacles in its path. Let's look at a few of those obstacles, to see what they are and how they work.

Growth requires learning. At times, it requires each of the types of learning discussed earlier. The most common barriers to growth are obstacles to the necessary learning experiences. If we think of growth as movement along a main path, these barriers divert us to cul-de-sacs. They keep us trapped there, or perhaps shuffle us from one to another. They can be characterized in different ways, but I find it convenient to group them in three main classes—infatuation, fear and failure to take responsibility.

As we grow, the way we view the world changes. We see it through different models and from different perspectives. For growth to continue, each of these stages must be transitory, replaced in its turn by the next. *Infatuation* with any particular stage can impede those transitions. We think "This is *IT* " and we try to hang on to and embellish that stage, blocking the changes that would diminish it and take us beyond.

Obvious examples of this syndrome include the "true believers" of all types, single-minded fanatics totally devoted to their cause, be it stamping out Communism; world revolution; making money; accumulating power, prestige and influence; or the latest "growth" therapy. Less obvious, but equally infatuated with his own limiting perspectives is the rational intellectual who accepts only precise terminology and logical argument, or the empirical scientist who only believes in things which can be quantified and observed in the laboratory.

These last two, in particular, exemplify the collective infatuations of contemporary society. Other societies with very different world-views have been equally infatuated with intuitive knowledge not consciously articulated and with magic as a way of manipulating the world. Either kind of infatuation can be equally limiting. This was the point of the Buddhist admonition against infatuation with paranormal powers mentioned earlier.

Infatuation is most obvious when it centers on a single explanatory model, blinding the perceiver to evidence which conflicts with that model and blocking the learning which accepting that evidence could bring. Examples include the medieval cleric unwilling to believe that the earth moves around the sun and the contemporary scientist unwilling to accept the existence of paranormal phenomena. But infatuation can also occur with a series of models or even with the transition from one to another. The individual models may each be revised in the face of new evidence, but the perceptual shift needed to move to a new level of understanding may be blocked.

Consider the "growth freaks" who move endlessly from one therapy or growth movement to another. With each shift they are convinced they have found *truth*, yet they soon become disillusioned and move on to seek *truth* in a new form. They never recognize that what they seek does not reside in the differences which distinguish the various movements but in the unseen underlying core common to them all.

In Western science infatuation with the ideas of "objective reality" and of the existence of a "best" way of describing that reality blocks the level shift necessary to see an underlying reality richer than any descriptive model. One scientific revolution follows another. Each produces a new "best" explanation to supersede the explanation preceding it and will itself be superseded by the explanation which follows. Yet many scientists are blind to the nature of this process, believing it to represent the steady accumulation of knowledge and movement toward truth.

Fear constitutes another major barrier to growth. It may be fear of something very specific—such as the economic uncertainty associated with a career change—or a more generalized fear of the unknown. It may be fear of moving away from a position which seems safe and secure to something new, or fear of change even when the current position is clearly untenable—like the fear of jumping off a runaway horse heading for a cliff. As children we all experienced fear's blocking growth—fear of the waves as we embark on our first adventure with the surf, or nervousness about our first date. Our parents, peers and our own need help us through these fears. We overcome them, get through the experiences, and in the process we learn and grow. But as we get older, fear becomes a more formidable barrier. We seem to have more at stake, and we find it easier to rationalize staying where we are and avoiding growth.

I knew a woman, for example, a "traditional housewife," who joined a consciousness-raising group in the early seventies when the women's movement was gaining steam. She began to reevaluate her life and her relationships with her husband and children. She saw that she did not have to live as she did; there could be different, better alternatives. At the same time, she doubted that she could ever bring her husband to share that vision and to accept the changes she saw were possible. She feared that if she continued to explore alternatives, she would reach a point where her existing life would become intolerable and her marriage would break up. That seemed too great a price to pay, so she quit the group.

I experienced similar fears as my own world-view began to broaden and to threaten the comfortable and secure niche I had made for myself. I then worked as a mathematician and systems analyst for the Rand Corporation, a "think tank" doing governmental policy studies. I was basically a believer in Western rationality and the scientific method, though somewhat dissatisfied with the way they were applied in systems analysis. I practiced T'ai Chi and Aikido as recreational activities and was becoming interested in the Oriental philosophies behind them.

My major research interest at that time concerned the

limitations of quantitative analysis in government policy studies and the misuses of analysis which resulted when appropriate limits were not observed. I was slowly moving away from the belief that the problems I saw were simply the result of carelessness and poor analysis; I was beginning to see fundamental flaws in the basic approach. I was coming to understand systems analysis in terms of perception—the institutional perceptions of bureaucratic organizations as well as the individual perceptions of systems analysts and their clients.

In the early seventies I began to see an increasing number of common threads running through my concerns about systems analysis as well as what I was learning from the martial arts and Oriental philosophy. I also discovered the writings of Carlos Castaneda and Joseph Pearce, who seemed to be dealing with the same basic ideas. They strengthened and reinforced my growing disenchantment with Western rationality and helped me to understand its limits and discover alternatives.

As all this was coming together, but still vague and indistinct, I realized I was facing an important choice. I could continue to explore these ideas and follow them where they led, or I could shut them off and stay with the world-view I was beginning to discard. The latter choice looked appealing in many ways. I didn't know where the former would lead, but even then it seemed clear that it would eventually threaten my ability to function as a conventional systems analyst and thus to make my living as I knew how. Economic security meant enough to me to make that prospect a little scary. Beyond that, I was calling some very basic beliefs into question without a very clear idea of what would replace them once they were gone. That was even more scary, then and many times since.

The new ideas and the potentials they opened up proved too interesting, and the former choice won out. Having made it, I could recognize others faced with similar choices and watch them make those choices. Some choose to go on, to grow in spite of the risk and uncertainty. Others choose to back off, to close off the avenues of doubt and to stay with the apparent security of their old world-view. I'm not trying to disparage that choice or to say that it's always the wrong one. But it may only delay the inevitable.

The final barrier I want to examine is the *failure to take responsibility*—for our own choices and for our own lives. One of the central ideas running through this book has concerned personal responsibility. We create our own realities by the choices we make in perceiving and interacting with the world around us. We make ourselves hungry, angry or sick—and we make ourselves well. We make many of these choices unconsciously through conditioned responses, to be sure. But we make them nonetheless. We are the only ones who can change such choices and make them differently.

That much responsibility can be very uncomfortable. So we create models of the world in which we have fewer choices and most of what happens to us results from forces beyond our control. Religious models in which events are the will of an omnipotent deity are like that, as is Western "objective reality" with its mechanistic "laws of nature." In the Western medical model illnesses are produced by external causes, while in many traditional models, they result from externally caused magic. This is not to deny the reality of "external events," nor to suggest that they have no influence on the situations we face. But the choices open to us in most situations are constrained far more by the limits we place on ourselves than by any external factors, as many of the earlier exercises have shown.

Our conditioning is strong and difficult to overcome. But overcoming that conditioning—taking conscious responsibility for our own lives—is what growth is all about. When we deny our own responsibility and attribute to external causes the limits we place on ourselves, we only make that process more difficult. These different barriers to growth are, of course, interrelated. Infatuation with a particular model of the world makes us afraid to let go of that model. The models we become infatuated with often explain what happens to us in terms of outside causes, so that in affirming them we deny our own responsibility. Once we have done so, taking that responsibility back, even to a limited extent, can be an awesome and fearful thing.

Our greatest fear may be that of acknowledging our own responsibility. But fearing it, denying it, cannot change it or make it go away. We are responsible, each one of us, and we each make our own reality. Growth is synonymous with accepting that responsibility, a bit at a time as we can handle it. We may delay and prolong the process, but in the long run we cannot avoid it.

As I said earlier, this is not a "how to" book, and I'm not going to offer you any particular methods or prescriptions for growth. There are plenty around, so if you're interested you should be able to find some which suit you. What this book should provide is an overview of the process and perhaps some help in making that choice more intelligently. To that end, I would like to close with some thoughts on the myriad of therapies, methods, movements and disciplines you have to choose from, and on what you might expect from them.

The main thing to remember is that *growth is an individual process*. Ultimately, you have to do it yourself. Disciplines, methods and the like can aid in that process, but only that. They are not the process, and they are not the goal. Different people are different; what works for me may not work for you and vice versa. There is no universal cure. What works for you at one time will get in the way at another. The concepts and methods which help you across one barrier become restrictive once you are past that barrier if you continue to hang on to them. According to a Buddhist metaphor you may need a raft to get across the river on your way to climb a mountain and find it of immeasurable value. But when you get to the other side, the raft has served its purpose. If you insist on lugging it up the mountainside, it can only impede your progress.

Movements and disciplines usually involve collective perceptual processes. They provide perceptual models through which their adherents may see the world. *All* collective perception—including science, culture and bureaucracy, as well as religious and growth movements—requires models simple enough for large groups of adherents to use and understand. Collective perceptions, for this reason, are usually more simplistic than intelligent individual perceptions.

A new movement or discipline may show you the world in a way that you have not seen before. As a result, it may show you a different world. But many movements fail to tell you that their world is no more "real" than the one you left. They may open a "crack" in your cosmic egg and help you to enlarge that crack. But they offer only another egg—different but equally enclosing. This is particularly true of disciplines which claim uniqueness—which claim to be better, and to offer more, than any other. "Your world is illusion," they may say, "but ours is real. Let us show it to you." The value in learning to see a different world lies, not in replacing the one you have, but in providing the basis for a level shift, a chance to see both from a larger perspective. As don Juan says in the Castaneda writings, the sorcerer's reality is as much an illusion as ordinary reality, but only when you can switch from one to the other at will can you really understand that.

This is not to suggest you should avoid growth movements or other aids to growth, by any means. They can offer important insights and learning experiences, and you can gain much from them. But you are your own best teacher and guide, the only one who knows *your* needs intimately. Listen to yourself, and learn to be sensitive to your own knowledge. In the final analysis, your growth is your own responsibility. You cannot delegate that responsibility to anyone else.

References

Boyd, Doug. *Rolling Thunder.* New York: Dell Publishing Co., 1974.

Castaneda, Carlos. *Journey to Ixtlan: The Lessons of Don Juan.* New York: Simon and Schuster, 1971.

Evans-Wentz, W. Y. *Tibetan Book of the Dead.* London: Oxford University Press, 1960.

Feldenkrais, Moshe. *Awareness through Movement.* New York: Harper and Row, 1972.

Gallwey, Tim. *The Inner Game of Tennis.* New York: Random House, 1976.

Hadamard, Jacques. *The Psychology of Invention in the Mathematical Field.* New York: Dover, 1954.

Herrigel, Eugene. *Zen and the Art of Archery.* New York: Pantheon, 1953.

Koestler, Arthur. *The Roots of Coincidence.* New York: Random House, 1972.

Kubler-Ross, Elizabeth. *Death: The Final Stage of Growth.* Englewood Cliffs, N.J.: Prentice-Hall, 1975.

Kuhn, Thomas. *The Structure of Scientific Revolution.* Chicago: University of Chicago Press, 1962.

Lao Tse, *Tao Te Ching.* The translation I like is Arthur Waley's *The Way and Its Power.* New York: Grove Press, 1958.

LeShan, Lawrence. *The Medium, the Mystic, and the Physicist: Toward a General Theory of the Paranormal.* New York: Viking, 1974.

Leonard, George. *The Ultimate Athlete: Re-Visioning Sports, Physical Education, and the Body.* New York: Viking Press, 1975.

Lilly, John. *The Mind of the Dolphin.* New York: Doubleday, 1967.

Monroe, Robert. *Journeys Out of the Body.* New York: Doubleday, 1971.

Moody, Raymond. *Life After Life.* New York: Bantam, 1975.

Neisser, Ulric. *Cognition and Reality.* San Francisco: W. H. Freeman & Co., 1976.

Ornstein, Robert. *The Psychology of Consciousness.* New York: Viking, 1974.

Pearce, Joseph Chilton. *Crack in the Cosmic Egg.* New York: Jullian, 1971.

Pirsig, Robert. *Zen and the Art of Motorcycle Maintenance.* New York: Bantam, 1975.

Roberts, Jane. *The Nature of Personal Reality.* Englewood Cliffs, N.J.: Prentice-Hall, 1974.

————. *Seth Speaks.* Englewood Cliffs, N.J.: Prentice-Hall, 1974.

Rose, Ronald. *Primitive Psychic Power.* New York: Rand McNally, 1956.

Roszak, Theodore. *Where the Wasteland Ends.* New York: Doubleday, 1972.

Simonton, Carl; Simonton, Stephanie; and Creighton, James. *Getting Well Again.* Los Angeles: J. P. Tarcher, 1978.

Storm, Hyemeyohsts. *Seven Arrows.* New York: Ballantine, 1972.

Whorf, Benjamin Lee. *Language, Thought, and Reality: Selected Writings of Benjamin Lee Whorf.* Boston: Technology Press of MIT, 1956.

Index

<u>Core Ideas</u>
10-11

Control
VII

Reality.
Illusion
P. 1-2
3\5

Issues of
Perception
12

Made in the USA
Lexington, KY
18 April 2012